#수능독해첫걸음
#내가바로독해강자

바로 읽는
배경지식 독해

바로 시리즈 검토에 도움을 주신 분들

홍정환 선생님(영어의 힘)
박용철 선생님(PK대치스마트에듀)
이성형 선생님(해윰학원)
주은숙 선생님(원클래스 학원)
윤지원 선생님(고려학원)
김지혜 선생님(Epic English)
채효석 선생님(빅터 아카데미)
박주경 선생님(PK대치스마트에듀)
원영아 선생님(멘토영어)
김란숙 선생님(샘앤아이영어)
김도희 선생님(원클래스 학원)
김현욱 선생님(동광학원)
박지혜 선생님(다이나믹 학원)
박은영 선생님(PK대치스마트에듀)
원지윤 선생님(아잉카영어)
이차은 선생님(BOB영어)
Kyle 선생님(한스터디)
이형언 선생님(훈성학원)
이민정 선생님(BMA 어학원)

원어민 검토

Stephanie Berry, Matthew D. Gunderman

Chunjae
Makes
Chunjae

[바로 읽는 배경지식 독해] LEVEL 2

기획총괄 장경률
편집개발 김윤미, 김희윤, 이민선
디자인총괄 김희정
표지디자인 윤순미, 안채리
내지디자인 디자인뮤제오
제작 황성진, 조규영

발행일 2022년 5월 15일 2판 2023년 10월 1일 2쇄
발행인 (주)천재교육
주소 서울시 금천구 가산로9길 54
신고번호 제2001-000018호
고객센터 1577-0902
교재 구입 문의 1522-5566

※ 정답 분실 시에는 천재교육 교재 홈페이지에서 내려받으세요.

중학부터 시작하는 수능 독해 첫걸음

바로 읽는 배경지식 독해

LEVEL 2

Draw Your Future Name Card

Picture Here

My Name ______________________

My Job ______________________

How to Use

영어 독해를 잘하기 위해서는 단순히 영어 문장만 읽을 줄 안다고 해서 다 되는 것이 아닙니다.
영어 문장을 읽어도 도무지 무슨 말인지 모르는 경우가 많기 때문입니다.

바로 읽는 배경지식 독해 시리즈는 여러분의 독해 실력 향상을 위해 다음과 같이 구성하였습니다.

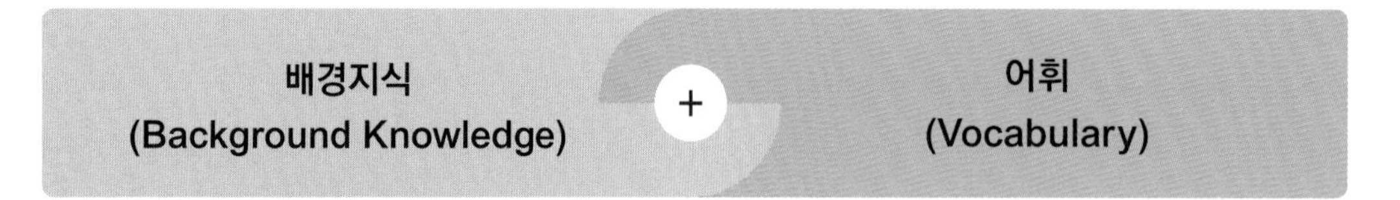

이 책을 통해 **배경지식**과 **어휘** 실력을 키워 나간다면,
수능 영어에서 출제되는 다양한 주제의 글들도 쉽게 이해할 수 있습니다.

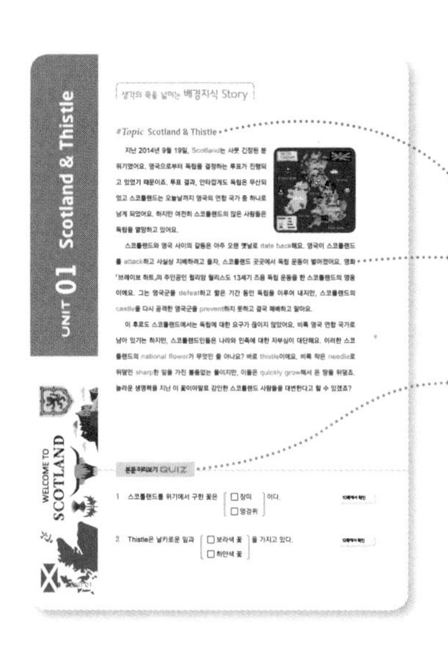

생각의 폭을 넓히는 배경지식 Story

- 재미있는 이야기를 통해, 주제에 관해 미리 생각해 보고 독해를 준비합니다.
- 읽을수록 어휘 실력도 향상됩니다. 잘 모르는 어휘는 Vocabulary에서 확인합니다.
- **본문 미리보기 QUIZ** 를 통해 배울 내용을 간단한 퀴즈로 미리 만나보세요.

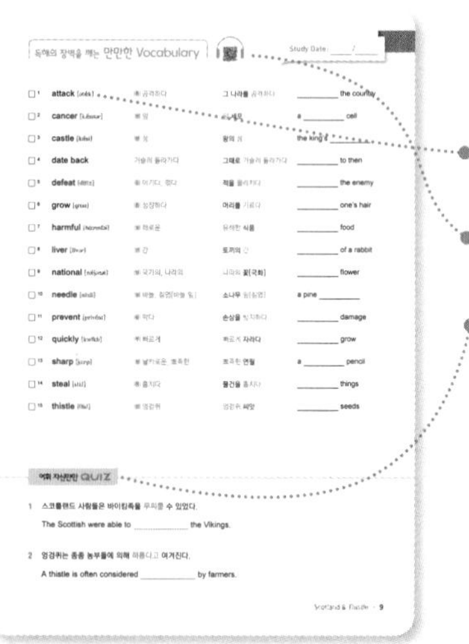

독해의 장벽을 깨는 만만한 Vocabulary

- 본문에 나오는 15개의 어휘를 미리 학습합니다.
- QR코드 제공: native speaker의 음성으로 단어를 들어보세요.
- **어휘 자신만만 QUIZ** 를 통해 실력을 간단히 체크합니다.

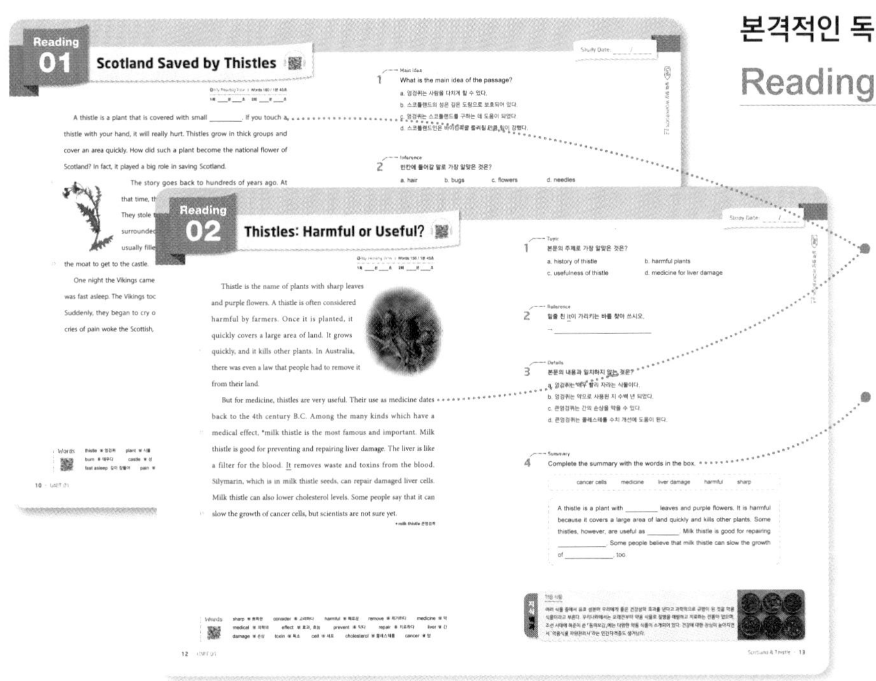

본격적인 독해 실력 향상을 위한 Reading 01, 02

- 1개의 Unit이 통합교과적 연관성을 지닌 두 개의 재미있는 이야기로 구성되어 있습니다.
- 체계적인 독해를 위한 main idea → details → summary 등과 같은 문제로 구성되어 있습니다.

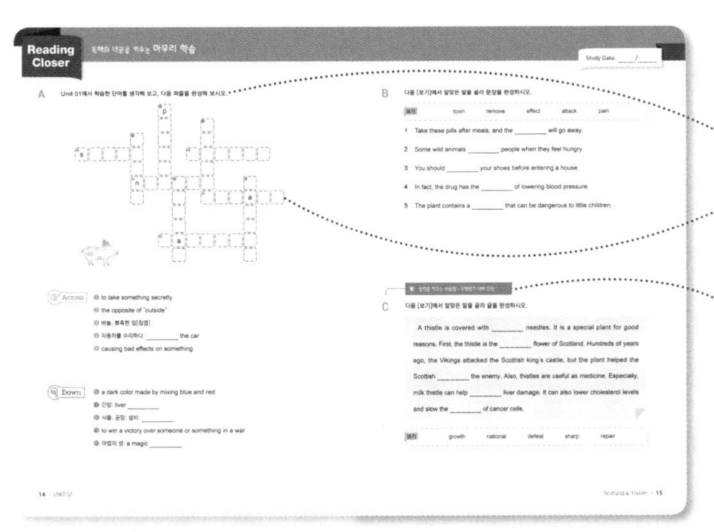

독해의 내공을 키우는 마무리 학습

- Unit에서 배운 어휘를 종합 점검합니다.
- crossword puzzle을 통한 재미있는 어휘 학습을 합니다.
- 생각을 키우는 서술형 · 수행평가 대비 훈련

앞에서 배운 2개의 Reading을 종합적으로 이해 및 평가합니다. 서술형 쓰기 연습을 통해 다양한 종류의 시험을 대비합니다.

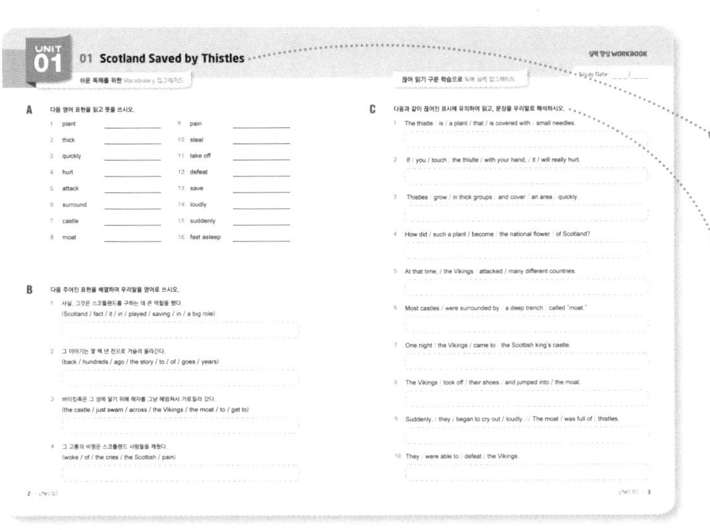

실력 향상 WORKBOOK

- 각 Reading마다 실력 향상을 위한 워크북이 제공됩니다.
- 쉬운 독해를 위한 Vocabulary와 끊어 읽기 구문 학습으로 여러분의 독해 실력을 한층 더 업그레이드 할 수 있습니다.

Table of Contents

LEVEL 2

LEVEL 2

Unit & Title	Reading	Category	Keyword	Words	Contents
09 Traveling Thailand	01. The Legend of Hanuman	신화	태국	161	태국에서 원숭이가 특별한 동물로 여겨지게 된 전설
	02. On the Elephant's Back	여행	태국	173	태국에서 코끼리 타기
10 Thank You, Gravity!	01. Muscles at Work	건강	근육	158	사람의 근육
	02. Exercise in Space	우주	무중력, 근육	171	우주 비행사들이 우주에서 운동을 해야 하는 이유와 방법
11 Home Alone	01. Living Alone	사회	현대 사회	174	1인 가구의 증가
	02. Convenience Foods	사회	현대 사회	155	즉석식품의 장점과 문제점
12 The Joy of Reading	01. Writing a Book Report	문학	책	175	좋은 독후감을 쓰는 방법
	02. Around the World in 80 Days	문학	책	176	「80일 간의 세계 일주」를 읽고 쓴 독후감
13 Interesting Math	01. Egyptian Way to Multiply	역사	수학	170	고대 이집트인들의 곱셈 방법
	02. Learning Multiplication	수학	곱셈	183	곱셈표의 흥미로운 패턴
14 Heal the World	01. If I Look at the One	심리학	기부	175	다수의 사람과 한 사람을 돕는 것에 대한 연구
	02. Knit One, Save One	사회, 봉사	기부	191	뜨개질로 만든 아기 모자 보내기 캠페인
15 Great Mayans	01. Pyramids in Mexico and Egypt	역사	피라미드	185	멕시코의 피라미드
	02. The Great Science of Mayans	수학	마야 문명	176	수학과 천문학이 발달한 마야 문명
16 The Armadillo's Song	01. How I Wish I Could Sing	문학	노래	176	음악을 사랑하는 아르마딜로의 이야기
	02. If I Die, I Can Sing	문학	노래	208	

"A room without books is like a body without a soul."

책 없는 방은 영혼 없는 육체와도 같다.

키케로 Cicero

Background Knowledge Reading

Self Study Management Table 자기 주도 학습 관리표

Unit	Start	Finish	Self Check				My Comment
	공부 시작	공부 끝	배경지식을 많이 쌓았어요!	어휘 실력이 늘었어요!	독해에 자신감이 +1 늘었어요!	모든 문제들을 다 풀었어요!	내 자신에게 한 마디!
01	월 일	월 일	☺ ☺ ☺	☺ ☺ ☺	☺ ☺ ☺	☺ ☺ ☺	
02	월 일	월 일	☺ ☺ ☺	☺ ☺ ☺	☺ ☺ ☺	☺ ☺ ☺	
03	월 일	월 일	☺ ☺ ☺	☺ ☺ ☺	☺ ☺ ☺	☺ ☺ ☺	
04	월 일	월 일	☺ ☺ ☺	☺ ☺ ☺	☺ ☺ ☺	☺ ☺ ☺	
05	월 일	월 일	☺ ☺ ☺	☺ ☺ ☺	☺ ☺ ☺	☺ ☺ ☺	
06	월 일	월 일	☺ ☺ ☺	☺ ☺ ☺	☺ ☺ ☺	☺ ☺ ☺	
07	월 일	월 일	☺ ☺ ☺	☺ ☺ ☺	☺ ☺ ☺	☺ ☺ ☺	
08	월 일	월 일	☺ ☺ ☺	☺ ☺ ☺	☺ ☺ ☺	☺ ☺ ☺	
09	월 일	월 일	☺ ☺ ☺	☺ ☺ ☺	☺ ☺ ☺	☺ ☺ ☺	
10	월 일	월 일	☺ ☺ ☺	☺ ☺ ☺	☺ ☺ ☺	☺ ☺ ☺	
11	월 일	월 일	☺ ☺ ☺	☺ ☺ ☺	☺ ☺ ☺	☺ ☺ ☺	
12	월 일	월 일	☺ ☺ ☺	☺ ☺ ☺	☺ ☺ ☺	☺ ☺ ☺	
13	월 일	월 일	☺ ☺ ☺	☺ ☺ ☺	☺ ☺ ☺	☺ ☺ ☺	
14	월 일	월 일	☺ ☺ ☺	☺ ☺ ☺	☺ ☺ ☺	☺ ☺ ☺	
15	월 일	월 일	☺ ☺ ☺	☺ ☺ ☺	☺ ☺ ☺	☺ ☺ ☺	
16	월 일	월 일	☺ ☺ ☺	☺ ☺ ☺	☺ ☺ ☺	☺ ☺ ☺	

My Comment에는 공부하고 나서 느낀 소감을 간단히 적어보세요.

중학부터 시작하는 수능 독해 첫걸음

바로 읽는 배경지식 독해

LEVEL 2

생각의 폭을 넓히는 배경지식 Story

#Topic Scotland & Thistle

지난 2014년 9월 19일, Scotland는 사뭇 긴장된 분위기였어요. 영국으로부터 독립을 결정하는 투표가 진행되고 있었기 때문이죠. 투표 결과, 안타깝게도 독립은 무산되었고 스코틀랜드는 오늘날까지 영국의 연합 국가 중 하나로 남게 되었어요. 하지만 여전히 스코틀랜드의 많은 사람들은 독립을 열망하고 있어요.

스코틀랜드와 영국 사이의 갈등은 아주 오랜 옛날로 date back해요. 영국이 스코틀랜드를 attack하고 사실상 지배하려고 들자, 스코틀랜드 곳곳에서 독립 운동이 벌어졌어요. 영화 「브레이브 하트」의 주인공인 윌리암 윌리스도 13세기 즈음 독립 운동을 한 스코틀랜드의 영웅이에요. 그는 영국군을 defeat하고 짧은 기간 동안 독립을 이루어 내지만, 스코틀랜드의 castle을 다시 공격한 영국군을 prevent하지 못하고 결국 패배하고 말아요.

이 후로도 스코틀랜드에서는 독립에 대한 요구가 끊이지 않았어요. 비록 영국 연합 국가로 남아 있기는 하지만, 스코틀랜드인들은 나라와 민족에 대한 자부심이 대단해요. 이러한 스코틀랜드의 national flower가 무엇인 줄 아나요? 바로 thistle이에요. 비록 작은 needle로 뒤덮인 sharp한 잎을 가진 볼품없는 풀이지만, 이들은 quickly grow해서 온 땅을 뒤덮죠. 놀라운 생명력을 지닌 이 꽃이야말로 강인한 스코틀랜드 사람들을 대변한다고 할 수 있겠죠?

본문 미리보기 QUIZ

1 스코틀랜드를 위기에서 구한 꽃은 [□ 장미 □ 엉겅퀴] 이다. 10쪽에서 확인

2 Thistle은 날카로운 잎과 [□ 보라색 꽃 □ 하얀색 꽃] 을 가지고 있다. 12쪽에서 확인

독해의 장벽을 깨는 만만한 Vocabulary

Study Date: ______ / ______

☐ 1	**attack** [ətǽk]	동 공격하다	그 나라를 공격하다	________ the country
☐ 2	**cancer** [kǽnsər]	명 암	암 세포	a ________ cell
☐ 3	**castle** [kǽsl]	명 성	왕의 성	the king's ________
☐ 4	**date back**	거슬러 올라가다	그때로 거슬러 올라가다	________ to then
☐ 5	**defeat** [difí:t]	동 이기다, 꺾다	적을 물리치다	________ the enemy
☐ 6	**grow** [grou]	동 성장하다	머리를 기르다	________ one's hair
☐ 7	**harmful** [há:rmfəl]	형 해로운	유해한 식품	________ food
☐ 8	**liver** [lívər]	명 간	토끼의 간	________ of a rabbit
☐ 9	**national** [nǽʃənəl]	형 국가의, 나라의	나라의 꽃[국화]	________ flower
☐ 10	**needle** [ní:dl]	명 바늘, 침엽[바늘 잎]	소나무 잎[침엽]	a pine ________
☐ 11	**prevent** [privént]	동 막다	손상을 방지하다	________ damage
☐ 12	**quickly** [kwíkli]	부 빠르게	빠르게 자라다	________ grow
☐ 13	**sharp** [ʃa:rp]	형 날카로운, 뾰족한	뾰족한 연필	a ________ pencil
☐ 14	**steal** [sti:l]	동 훔치다	물건을 훔치다	________ things
☐ 15	**thistle** [θísl]	명 엉겅퀴	엉겅퀴 씨앗	________ seeds

어휘 자신만만 QUIZ

1 스코틀랜드 사람들은 바이킹족을 무찌를 수 있었다.

The Scottish were able to ________ the Vikings.

2 엉겅퀴는 종종 농부들에 의해 해롭다고 여겨진다.

A thistle is often considered ________ by farmers.

Reading 01

Scotland Saved by Thistles

My Reading Time | Words 160 / 1분 45초

1회 ____분 ____초 2회 ____분 ____초

A thistle is a plant that is covered with small __________. If you touch a thistle with your hand, it will really hurt. Thistles grow in thick groups and cover an area quickly. How did such a plant become the national flower of Scotland? In fact, it played a big role in saving Scotland.

The story goes back to hundreds of years ago. At that time, the Vikings attacked many different countries. They stole things and burned castles. Most castles were surrounded by a deep *trench called a "moat." It was usually filled with water. The Vikings just swam across the moat to get to the castle.

One night the Vikings came to the Scottish king's castle. Everyone inside was fast asleep. The Vikings took off their shoes and jumped into the moat. Suddenly, they began to cry out loudly. The moat was full of thistles. The cries of pain woke the Scottish, and they were able to defeat the Vikings.

*trench 성 둘레의 구덩이

Words

thistle 명 엉겅퀴 plant 명 식물 thick 형 두꺼운, 울창한 attack 동 공격하다 steal 동 훔치다
burn 동 태우다 castle 명 성 surround 동 둘러싸다 moat 명 해자[성 주위의 깊은 연못]
fast asleep 깊이 잠들어 pain 명 아픔, 통증 defeat 동 이기다, 꺾다

LINK 실력 향상 WORKBOOK p.2

1 Main Idea

What is the main idea of the passage?

a. 엉겅퀴는 사람을 다치게 할 수 있다.

b. 스코틀랜드의 성은 깊은 도랑으로 보호되어 있다.

c. 엉겅퀴는 스코틀랜드를 구하는 데 도움이 되었다.

d. 스코틀랜드인은 바이킹족을 물리칠 만큼 힘이 강했다.

2 Inference

빈칸에 들어갈 말로 가장 알맞은 것은?

a. hair   b. bugs   c. flowers   d. needles

3 Details

바이킹족이 크게 비명을 지른 이유로 가장 알맞은 것은?

a. They wanted to wake up the Scottish.

b. The moat was too deep to swim across.

c. They stepped on thistles without shoes.

d. The Scottish were waiting to attack them.

4 Graphic Organizer

본문의 단어를 이용하여 줄거리를 완성하시오.

The Vikings came to attack the Scottish king's ___________.

They jumped into the moat. It was full of ___________.

They cried out loudly.

The Scottish woke up and could ___________ the Vikings.

지식백과

에든버러성

현재 스코틀랜드에는 600개가 넘는 성(castle)이 있으며, 가장 유명한 성은 에든버러의 Castle Rock이라는 바위산에 세워진 Edinburgh Castle이다. 12세기부터 1633년까지 스코틀랜드의 왕족이 살던 곳으로, 과거에는 '해자'(moat)라고 불리는 깊은 도랑이 성을 에워싸고 있었지만 현재는 남아 있지 않다. 성 안에는 스코틀랜드의 왕이 대관식 때 왕관을 받기 위해 무릎을 꿇던 '운명의 돌(The Stone of Destiny)'이 있다. 이 돌은 한 때 잉글랜드에 빼앗겼다가 1996년에 돌려받은 것이다. 일요일을 제외한 매일 오후 1시에 대포를 쏘는 것으로 유명하다.

해자가 있는 세계의 성을 동영상으로 감상해 보세요. Time 3' 46"

Reading
02

Thistles: Harmful or Useful?

My Reading Time | Words 156 / 1분 45초

1회 ____분____초 2회 ____분____초

Thistle is the name of plants with sharp leaves and purple flowers. A thistle is often considered harmful by farmers. Once it is planted, it quickly covers a large area of land. It grows quickly, and it kills other plants. In Australia, there was even a law that people had to remove it from their land.

But for medicine, thistles are very useful. Their use as medicine dates back to the 4th century B.C. Among the many kinds which have a medical effect, *milk thistle is the most famous and important. Milk thistle is good for preventing and repairing liver damage. The liver is like a filter for the blood. It removes waste and toxins from the blood. Silymarin, which is in milk thistle seeds, can repair damaged liver cells. Milk thistle can also lower cholesterol levels. Some people say that it can slow the growth of cancer cells, but scientists are not sure yet.

* **milk thistle** 큰엉겅퀴

Words

sharp 형 뾰족한 consider 동 고려하다 harmful 형 해로운 remove 동 제거하다 medicine 명 약
medical 형 의학의 effect 명 효과, 효능 prevent 동 막다 repair 동 치료하다 liver 명 간
damage 명 손상 toxin 명 독소 cell 명 세포 cholesterol 명 콜레스테롤 cancer 명 암

LINK 실력 향상 WORKBOOK p.4

1 Topic

본문의 주제로 가장 알맞은 것은?

a. history of thistle
b. harmful plants
c. usefulness of thistle
d. medicine for liver damage

2 Reference

밑줄 친 It이 가리키는 바를 찾아 쓰시오.

→ ______________________

3 Details

본문의 내용과 일치하지 않는 것은?

a. 엉겅퀴는 매우 빨리 자라는 식물이다.
b. 엉겅퀴는 약으로 사용된 지 수백 년 되었다.
c. 큰엉겅퀴는 간의 손상을 막을 수 있다.
d. 큰엉겅퀴는 콜레스테롤 수치 개선에 도움이 된다.

4 Summary

Complete the summary with the words in the box.

cancer cells	medicine	liver damage	harmful	sharp

A thistle is a plant with __________ leaves and purple flowers. It is harmful because it covers a large area of land quickly and kills other plants. Some thistles, however, are useful as __________. Milk thistle is good for repairing ______________. Some people believe that milk thistle can slow the growth of ______________, too.

지식 백과

약용 식물

여러 식물 중에서 유효 성분이 우리에게 좋은 건강상의 효과를 낸다고 과학적으로 규명이 된 것을 약용 식물이라고 부른다. 우리나라에서는 오래전부터 약용 식물로 질병을 예방하고 치료하는 전통이 있으며, 조선 시대에 허준이 쓴 「동의보감」에는 다양한 약용 식물이 소개되어 있다. 건강에 대한 관심이 높아지면서 '약용식물 자원관리사'라는 민간자격증도 생겨났다.

Reading Closer

독해의 내공을 키우는 마무리 학습

A Unit 01에서 학습한 단어를 생각해 보고, 다음 퍼즐을 완성해 보시오.

❶ s
❸ n
❹ a
❺ a
❻ p

Across

❶ to take something secretly

❷ the opposite of "outside"

❸ 바늘, 뾰족한 잎[침엽]

❹ 자동차를 수리하다: ________ the car

❺ causing bad effects on something

Down

❻ a dark color made by mixing blue and red

❼ 간암: liver ________

❽ 식물; 공장; 설비: ________

❾ to win a victory over someone or something in a war

❿ 마법의 성: a magic ________

B 다음 [보기]에서 알맞은 말을 골라 문장을 완성하시오.

보기	toxin	remove	effect	attack	pain

1 Take these pills after meals, and the __________ will go away.

2 Some wild animals __________ people when they feel hungry.

3 You should __________ your shoes before entering a house.

4 In fact, the drug has the __________ of lowering blood pressure.

5 The plant contains a __________ that can be dangerous to little children.

생각을 키우는 서술형 • 수행평가 대비 훈련

C 다음 [보기]에서 알맞은 말을 골라 글을 완성하시오.

A thistle is covered with __________ needles. It is a special plant for good reasons. First, the thistle is the __________ flower of Scotland. Hundreds of years ago, the Vikings attacked the Scottish king's castle, but the plant helped the Scottish __________ the enemy. Also, thistles are useful as medicine. Especially, milk thistle can help __________ liver damage. It can also lower cholesterol levels and slow the __________ of cancer cells.

보기	growth	national	defeat	sharp	repair

생각의 폭을 넓히는 **배경지식 Story**

#Topic Cell Phones

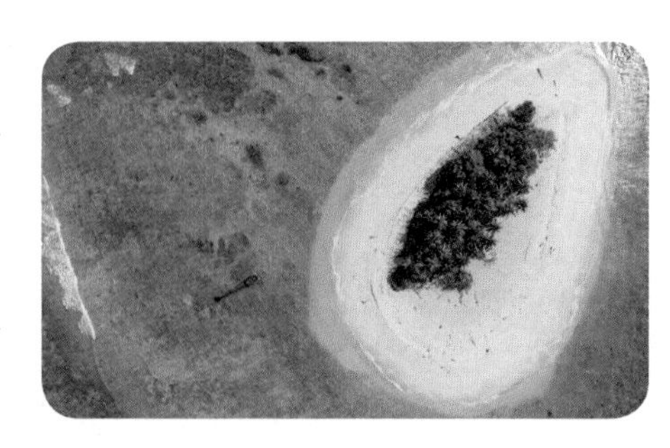

여러분이 무인도에 가게 된다면 챙겨가고 싶은 세 가지는? 대부분의 사람이 적어도 하나는 cell phone을 생각할 거예요. 휴대 전화가 점점 똑똑해짐에 따라 온갖 function을 수행할 수 있어요. 전화를 걸거나 receive하여 멀리 있는 친구들과 contact를 유지하는 것은 기본이고, 음악이나 영화, 게임 등의 entertainment를 즐길 수도 있죠. 그래서 휴대 전화는 오늘날 우리의 necessity가 되었어요.

휴대 전화는 우리의 삶에 positive한 영향을 주고 있어요. 언제 어디서나 정보를 검색할 수 있기 때문에 우리는 모든 것을 다 암기할 필요가 없어졌어요. 따라서 더 많은 시간과 노력을 고차원적인 부분에 투자할 수 있게 되었어요. 게다가 사람과 사람 사이를 connect하는 social 관계망 서비스(SNS)를 이용하여 언제 어디서나 사람들과 communicate를 할 수 있기 때문에 더 개방적인 사회를 만드는 데 도움을 주기도 하죠.

하지만 휴대 전화 혹은 스마트폰이 정말 우리를 '스마트'하게 해 주는지에 대해 의심하는 사람들도 많아요. 이 작지만 영리한 tool에 우리가 너무 의지하기 때문에, 간단한 셈을 하거나 친한 사람의 전화번호도 기억하지 못하는 경우가 있어요. 이러한 현상을 디지털 치매라고 불러요. 그럼 이제, 휴대 전화에 관한 다양한 이야기들을 함께 시작해 볼까요?

본문 미리보기 QUIZ

1 최근 연구 사례는 휴대 전화의 [□ 전자파 / □ 중독] 이/가 문제임을 보여 준다. 18쪽에서 확인

2 1990년대 초 휴대 전화는 평균적으로 [□ 벽돌 / □ 바구니] 정도의 크기였다. 20쪽에서 확인

UNIT 02 Cell Phones

독해의 장벽을 깨는 만만한 Vocabulary

Study Date: ____ / ____

□ 1	**addicted** [ədíktid]	형 중독된	중독되다	become ________
□ 2	**brick** [brik]	명 벽돌	벽돌 집	a ________ house
□ 3	**communicate** [kəmjúːnəkèit]	동 의사소통하다	그와 연락을 주고받다	________ with him
□ 4	**connect** [kənékt]	동 연결하다	사람들과 연결하다	________ with people
□ 5	**contact** [kɑ́ntækt]	명 연락, 접촉	연락을 유지하다	stay in ________
□ 6	**entertainment** [èntərtéinmənt]	명 오락	오락을 제공하다	provide ________
□ 7	**function** [fʌ́ŋkʃən]	명 기능	기능을 수행하다	perform a ________
□ 8	**luxury** [lʌ́kʃəri]	명 사치(품)	호화 호텔	a ________ hotel
□ 9	**necessity** [nəsésəti]	명 필수(품)	생활 필수품	a daily ________
□ 10	**positive** [pɑ́zətiv]	형 긍정적인	긍정적인 효과	________ effects
□ 11	**receive** [risíːv]	동 받다	전화를 받다	________ calls
□ 12	**record** [rikɔ́ːrd]	동 녹음하다, 기록하다	행사를 기록하다	________ events
□ 13	**social** [sóuʃəl]	형 사회의	사회적 문제	________ problems
□ 14	**sweat** [swet]	명 땀	식은땀	a cold ________
□ 15	**tool** [tuːl]	명 도구	유용한 도구	a useful ________

어휘 자신만만 QUIZ

1 어떤 사람들은 자신의 휴대 전화에 중독되었다.

Some people became ____________ to their cell phones.

2 여러분은 문자를 보내거나 목소리를 녹음할 수 있다.

You can send text messages or ____________ voices.

Reading 01

Addicted to Cell Phones

My Reading Time | Words 160 / 1분 45초

1회 ____분____초 2회 ____분____초

Would you be upset if you could not use your cell phone at school? Do you break out in a cold sweat when your cell phone battery dies? If you cannot live without your cell phone, you might have a problem.

A recent study found that some people could be addicted to their cell phones. About 40 percent of students said they could not live without their cell phones. About 90 percent said they took their phones with them everywhere. The study shows that students use their phones a lot. This has some positive effects such as staying in contact with friends. But sending all those text messages or doing all sorts of things online costs time and money.

As part of the study, some students agreed to take a break from their cell phones. After three phone-free days, students said that ________________ ________________. That might be a good reason to hang up the phone!

Words upset 형 속상한 cell phone 휴대 전화 break out 발생하다 cold sweat 식은땀 recent 형 최근의 addicted 형 중독된 positive 형 긍정적인 contact 명 연락, 접촉 all sorts of 모든 종류의 take a break 휴식을 취하다 hang up 전화를 끊다

LINK 실력 향상 WORKBOOK p.6

Main Idea

1 What is the main idea of the passage?

a. 휴대 전화는 학생들에게 유용하다.

b. 휴대 전화는 많은 긍정적 효과를 가진다.

c. 학교에서 휴대 전화 사용을 금지해야 한다.

d. 많은 학생들이 휴대 전화에 중독되어 있다.

Inference

2 빈칸에 들어갈 말로 가장 알맞은 것은?

a. they felt freer than before

b. the survey results were wrong

c. they couldn't contact their families

d. they wanted to buy a new cell phone

Details

3 본문의 내용과 일치하도록 빈칸에 알맞은 말을 쓰시오.

Q: What are the bad things about using cell phones too much?

A: Sending __________ __________ or doing things __________ costs time and money.

Summary

4 Complete the summary with the words in the box.

three	used	addicted	positive	bad	four

Some people might be __________ to their cell phones. A recent study showed that many students __________ their phones a lot. This has not only __________ effects but also negative ones. Some students took a break from their cell phones for __________ days. They felt less stressed.

지식백과

휴대 전화의 블루라이트

모니터, 휴대 전화, 텔레비전 등에서 나오는 파란색 계열의 빛을 블루라이트라고 부르며, 380~500nm 사이의 파장에 존재하는 빛이다. 블루라이트에 장시간 노출되면 눈이 피로해지고, 안구 건조증이 발생하며, 수면 유도 호르몬 분비가 제대로 되지 않아 수면 장애를 겪을 수 있다. 블루라이트의 잠재적 유해성이 인식되면서 각종 차단 필름, 소프트웨어 및 시력 보호 모니터 등이 개발·보급되고 있다.

블루라이트에 관한 뉴스를 시청해 보세요. Time 1' 53"

Reading 02

Cell Phones: How Smart!

My Reading Time | Words 160 / 1분 50초

1회 ____분____초 2회 ____분____초

Not so long ago, cell phones were a luxury, not a necessity. It is hard to imagine now, but in the early 1990s the average cell phone was as big as a brick and only had one function: to make and receive calls.

Cell phones have changed the way we talk to each other. We can communicate with text messages. We can also take photos and share them with other people. Cell phone makers are adding new functions every day. We can exchange e-mail, play games, watch movies, record events, pay for bus rides, and connect with others using a social networking service. Of course, we can still talk on them. All of this is in one tiny box.

People of nearly all ages have really started to think of cell phones in different ways. They regard cell phones not only as a communication tool, but also as an important source of entertainment. They feel they cannot live without them.

Words

luxury 명 사치품 necessity 명 필수품 brick 명 벽돌 function 명 기능 receive 동 받다 record 동 기록하다 pay 동 지불하다 connect 동 연결하다 social networking service 사회 관계망 서비스(SNS) tiny 형 작은 tool 명 도구 source 명 원천, 근원 entertainment 명 오락

LINK 실력 향상 WORKBOOK p.8

1 Title

본문의 두 번째 단락의 제목으로 가장 알맞은 것은?

a. The History of Cell Phones

b. Various Functions of Cell Phones

c. The Good Effects of Using Cell Phones

d. How to Add New Functions to Cell Phones

2 Words

밑줄 친 one tiny box가 가리키는 바로 가장 알맞은 것은?

a. SNS   b. cell phone   c. one function   d. entertainment

3 Details

문장을 읽고 본문의 내용과 일치하면 T, 일치하지 않으면 F를 쓰시오.

(1) _____ Early cell phones were much bigger than today's phones.

(2) _____ Cell phone makers are adding new functions.

(3) _____ Younger people only use cell phones for entertainment.

4 Graphic Organizer

본문의 단어를 이용하여 휴대전화로 할 수 있는 작업을 완성하시오.

With cell phones, we can ....

- talk
- use a social networking service
- pay for bus rides
- (5) __________ events
- watch movies
- (4) play __________
- (3) send and receive __________
- (2) take __________
- (1) send __________ messages

지식 백과

기술 발달의 폐해, 전자쓰레기

사용자가 수명이 다하여 버린 전기·전자제품을 뜻하며, 텔레비전 등 대형 가전제품에서부터 휴대 전화와 같은 소형 전자 제품에 이르기까지 다양한 폐기물을 포함한다. 급속한 기술 발달과 소비자의 새로운 것에 대한 욕구 때문에 전 세계적으로 이러한 폐기물이 넘쳐나고 있으며, 이로 인해 환경 파괴가 가속화되고 있다.

A Unit 02에서 학습한 단어를 생각해 보고, 다음 퍼즐을 완성해 보시오.

Across

❶ 식은땀을 흘리다: break out in a cold ________

❷ 친구들과 연락하며 지내다: stay in ________ with friends

❸ She has become ________ to online games.
(그녀는 온라인 게임에 중독되어 가고 있다.)

❹ 전화를 끊다: ________ up

Down

❺ 문자 메시지를 받다: receive ________ messages

❻ The heart's ________ is to pump blood.

❼ ________ A as B: A를 B로 간주하다

❽ 평균의

❾ 도구 상자: a ________ box

❿ 현금으로 지불하다: ________ in cash

Study Date: ______ / ______

B 다음 [보기]에서 알맞은 말을 골라 문장을 완성하시오.

보기	imagine	source	recent	positive	share

1 Oranges and other fruits are a good __________ of vitamin C.

2 In our apartment, I __________ a room with my brother.

3 Regular exercise has many __________ effects on health.

4 The writer has surprising ability to __________ things.

5 Vegetable prices have risen sharply in __________ months.

생각을 키우는 서술형 • 수행평가 대비 훈련

C 다음 네모 안에서 알맞은 말을 골라 글을 완성하시오.

Many teens seem to be [added / addicted] to cell phones. They take their phones with them everywhere to listen to music, watch movies, or stay in [contact / connect] with their friends. For them, cell phones are not a [product / luxury], but a necessity. They are expected to use cell phones more because new [functions / buttons] are added to them fast. By using the [average / tiny] tool, they will be able to do almost anything in the years to come.

UNIT 03 Light & Shadow

생각의 폭을 넓히는 **배경지식 Story**

#Topic Shadows

여러분을 wherever 따라다니지만 우리가 잘 눈치채지 못하는 것은? 바로 우리의 shadow예요. 잘 알고 있듯이 그림자는 빛이 어떤 object에 닿을 때 form하게 되는 어두운 부분이에요. 다양한 angle에 따라 shadow의 모양도 달라지죠.

독일 작가 폰 샤미소의 작품 「페터 슐레밀의 기이한 이야기」는 페터 슐레밀이라는 사람이 자신의 shadow를 팔고 나서 겪은 이야기를 들려줘요. 어느 날 정체를 알 수 없는 회색 신사가 슐레밀에게 shadow를 팔면 황금 주머니를 주겠다고 제안을 하죠. shadow가 아무런 쓸모 없다고 생각한 슐레밀은 shadow를 팔고 부자가 되죠. 그림자는 정말 아무런 쓸모가 없는 것이었을까요?

그림자가 없어지자 많은 사람들이 슐레밀을 피해 다녔어요. In addition, 슐레밀은 아름다운 아가씨와 사랑에 빠졌는데, 그가 그림자가 없다는 사실을 안 그녀는 그만 떠나고 말죠. 그림자가 없는 사람이라니! 사람이라고 할 수 있을까요? 결국 슐레밀은 다시 찾아온 greedy한 신사에게 자신의 그림자를 돌려달라고 부탁하죠. opposite한 상황이 되고 만 것이죠. 하지만 악마에게 영혼을 팔아야만 돌려받을 수 있다는 말에 그만 포기하고 말아요. 마지막 양심까지 버릴 수는 없었으니까요.

이 신기한 이야기에 나오는 그림자는 무슨 의미일까요? 인간답게 보이게 하는 것, 인간의 도덕성, 양심, 자유 의지 등 여러 가지로 해석이 될 것 같아요. 이번 시간에는 이렇듯 늘 우리 곁에 있는 그림자에 대해 좀 더 알아보기로 해요.

본문 미리보기 QUIZ

1 탐욕스러운 남자가 판 것은 [☐ 나무 / ☐ 담장] 의 그림자이다. 26쪽에서 확인

2 태양에 의해 생기는 그림자가 가장 짧을 때는 [☐ 정오 / ☐ 해 질 녘] 이다. 28쪽에서 확인

독해의 장벽을 깨는 만만한 Vocabulary

Study Date: ______ / ______

□ 1	addition [ədíʃən]	명 추가, 부가	추가로	in ________
□ 2	angle [ǽŋgl]	명 각도	다른 각도에서	at different ________s
□ 3	belong [bilɔ́:ŋ]	동 ~에 속하다	그의 것이다	________ to him
□ 4	block [blak]	동 막다, 가리다	길을 막다	________ the path
□ 5	contrast [kántræst]	명 대조, 대비	대조적으로	in ________
□ 6	form [fɔ:rm]	동 형성하다	별 모양을 형성하다	________ a star shape
□ 7	greedy [grí:di]	형 욕심 많은	욕심 많은 사람들	________ people
□ 8	object [ábdʒikt]	명 물건	아주 작은 물건	a tiny ________
□ 9	opposite [ápəzit]	형 반대의	반대 쪽	the ________ side
□ 10	path [pæθ]	명 길, 통로	길을 따라서	along the ________
□ 11	rotate [róuteit]	동 회전하다	회전하기 시작하다	start to ________
□ 12	shade [ʃeid]	명 그늘, 응달	나무의 그늘	the ________ of a tree
□ 13	shadow [ʃǽdou]	명 그림자	내 자신의 그림자	my own ________
□ 14	sunset [sʌ́nsèt]	명 해 질 녘	해 질 녘에	at ________
□ 15	wherever [hwɛərévər]	접 어디든지	네가 가는 어디든지	________ you go

어휘 자신만만 QUIZ

1 내가 당신으로부터 그림자를 샀으므로, 이제 그것은 나의 소유이다.

I bought the shadow from you, so it now ________ to me.

2 어떤 물체가 빛이 가는 길을 막을 때, 그림자가 생긴다.

When an object blocks light's ________, a shadow is formed.

Reading
01 Whose Shadow Is It?

My Reading Time | Words 179 / 2분 00초

1회 ____분____초 2회 ____분____초

Once upon a time there lived a greedy man in a small village. On a hot summer day, a boy was passing by the village. The boy rested in the shade of the tree next to the man's house. When the man saw the boy, he said, "Hey, my grandfather planted this tree, so its shadow belongs to me."

5 (A) The boy got angry and decided to do something. He asked the man to sell the shadow to him. The man agreed. At sunset, the shadow of the tree was inside the man's yard. The boy walked in and lay there. (B) The man told the boy to leave, but he answered, "I bought this shadow from you, so it now belongs to me."

10 (C) When the shadow was inside the man's room, the boy walked in and lay there. The greedy man couldn't say anything. (D) He asked the boy to sell the shadow back to him. He had to pay the boy three times the original price.

Words

shadow 명 그림자 greedy 형 욕심 많은 pass by ~을 지나가다 rest 동 쉬다 shade 명 그늘 belong to ~에게 속하다 decide to ~을 결심하다 sunset 명 해 질 녘 yard 명 마당 lie 동 눕다(과거형 lay) original 형 본래의

LINK 실력 향상 WORKBOOK p.10

Title

1 본문의 다른 제목으로 가장 알맞은 것은?

a. Problems in a Small Village

b. Good Things About Shadows

c. A Greedy Man and a Clever Boy

d. How to Keep Cool in the Summer

Organization

2 주어진 문장이 들어가기에 가장 알맞은 곳은?

> After the boy repeated this for several days, the man couldn't stand it anymore.

a. (A)   b. (B)   c. (C)   d. (D)

Details

3 문장을 읽고 본문의 내용과 일치하면 T, 일치하지 않으면 F를 쓰시오.

(1) ______ The greedy man planted the tree.

(2) ______ The boy followed the shadow into the greedy man's house.

(3) ______ The greedy man bought three shadows from the boy.

Summary

4 Complete the summary with the words in the box.

house	shadow	tree	rest	next to	under

On a hot summer day, a boy wanted to __________ in the shade of the tree __________ a greedy man's house. However, the man didn't let the boy do that. The boy got angry and bought the __________. He followed the shadow everywhere, even into the man's __________. After all, the man had to buy back the shadow at a much higher price.

지식백과

민사 소송이란?

개인 간의 다툼을 법적으로 해결하는 방법이 민사 소송이다. 형사 소송과는 달리 민사 소송은 권리를 주장하는 사람이 법원에 소송을 내야 그 절차가 시작되는데, 이때 법원에 제출하는 서류가 '소장'이다. 소장에는 원고(소송을 제기하는 사람)가 피고(소송을 당하는 사람)에게 무엇을 어떤 근거로 청구하는지를 밝혀야 한다. 민사 소송에서 판사는 원고와 피고의 주장과 증거를 바탕으로 누구 말이 맞는지 판결한다.

Reading 02

Light Makes Shadow

My Reading Time | Words 164 / 1분 50초

1회 ___분 ___초 2회 ___분 ___초

Our shadow is a friend who always follows us around. When there is light, it stays with us wherever we go. Have you ever wondered how a shadow is formed? The answer is in the nature of light. Light travels in a straight line. When an object blocks its path, a shadow is formed on the opposite side. If there are many sources of light, we can see many shadows around the same object.

In addition, our shadow is a friend who changes its size. It can be very long or very short. For example, when the sun is rising in the east, our shadow is quite long. Even a short person has a long shadow. In contrast, the shadow is very short at noon when the sun is high in the sky. Even a tall person has a short shadow. As the Earth rotates during the day, the sunlight falls on us at different angles. This causes the shadow to change its size.

Words

wherever 접 어디든지 form 동 형성하다 nature 명 성질, 본성 object 명 물건 block 동 막다 path 명 길, 통로 opposite 형 반대의 source 명 근원, 원천 in addition 게다가 quite 부 매우, 아주 in contrast 그에 반해서 rotate 동 회전하다 angle 명 각도

LINK 실력 향상 WORKBOOK p.12

1

Topic

What is the passage mainly about?

a. the nature of light

b. different sources of light

c. the role of light in forming shadows

d. ways to measure the length of a shadow

2

Words

밑줄 친 path의 뜻으로 가장 알맞은 것은?

a. way　　b. source　　c. shadow　　d. light

3

Details

본문의 내용과 일치하는 것은?

a. A shadow is formed when light is weak.

b. There are more shadows than sources of light.

c. Shadows look longer or shorter at different times of the day.

d. Light falls on us at different angles, so shadows grow taller and taller.

4

Graphic Organizer

본문의 단어를 이용하여 표를 완성하시오.

Light travels in a __________ line.

When it meets an __________, a shadow is formed.	In the morning, the shadow is __________.	At noon, the shadow is __________.

지식백과

해시계: 앙부일구

앙부일구는 그 모양이 마치 '하늘을 우러러 보는 가마솥과 같은 해시계'라고 해서 붙여진 이름이다. 특히 오목한 모양의 해시계는 세계적으로도 유래를 찾기 힘든 독특한 것으로, 1434년에 장영실, 이천, 김조 등이 참여하여 만들었다. 이 해시계를 통해 백성들은 계절과 시각을 쉽게 알 수 있었다. 하지만 세종 때 만들어진 앙부일구는 임진왜란 때에 모두 없어졌고, 17세기 후반~18세기에 다시 만들어졌다. 보물 제845호로 지정되어 있다.

앙부일구로 시간을 어떻게 측정했는지 동영상으로 살펴보세요. Time 0' 45"

Reading Closer

독해의 내공을 키우는 **마무리 학습**

A Unit 03에서 학습한 단어를 생각해 보고, 다음 퍼즐을 완성해 보시오.

Across

❶ The Earth ________s round the sun.

❷ 본래의 계획: the ________ plan

❸ 해 질 녘

❹ 꽤, 상당히

Down

❺ 그에 반해서: in ________

❻ ~의 것이다[소유이다]: ________ to

❼ having a strong or great desire for food or wealth

❽ the form of energy that makes it possible to see things

❾ to make something happen or exist

❿ Mike was looking at his ________.
(Mike는 그의 그림자를 바라보고 있었다.)

Study Date: ____ / ____

B 다음 [보기]에서 알맞은 말을 골라 문장을 완성하시오.

보기 block angle rest agree original

1 You should try to look at the problem from another ________.

2 The athlete was so tired that he wanted to ________ on a sofa.

3 Lots of people complained, so the city changed its ________ plan.

4 As the singer left the court, the crowd tried to ________ his way.

5 When two people do not ________ about something, they may get into an argument.

생각을 키우는 서술형 • 수행평가 대비 훈련

C 다음 [보기]에서 알맞은 말을 골라 글을 완성하시오.

I think that the story about a boy and a ________ man is based on science. They argued about the shadow of a tree. The man did not know how light and ________ work. However, the boy understood the role of light in ________ shadows. He knew well that shadows are with us wherever we go when there is a ________ of light. He also knew that shadows change sizes as the Earth ________ during the day.

보기 rotates shadows forming source greedy

생각의 폭을 넓히는 배경지식 Story

#*Topic* Hot Air Balloon

터키의 카파도키아는 여러 가지 모양의 암석들이 여행객들을 불러 모으는 유명한 관광지예요. 그런데 관광객들은 이 지역의 암석을 보기 위해서 아주 특이한 것을 탄다고 해요. 바로 hot air balloon이에요!

특별히 카파도키아에서 열기구를 관광에 사용하는 데는 몇 가지 이유가 있어요. 먼저 이 지역의 높이 솟아 있는 기암괴석을 제대로 감상하기 위해서는 위에서 아래로 내려다보는 열기구가 가장 좋은 탈 것이라고 해요. 게다가 이 지역의 대기 layer는 항상 still해서 1년 내내 열기구를 띄우기에 안성맞춤이지요. 그에 반해 temperature가 급격히 변하거나 대기가 자주 unstable하다면 열기구를 띄울 수 있는 날이 제한되겠죠.

열기구를 띄우는 principle은 간단해요. 뜨거운 공기는 위로 가고, 차가운 공기는 sink되는 원리를 이용해요. 열기구의 기낭 또는 가스주머니에 뜨거운 공기를 넣으면 열기구가 float하는 거죠. passenger는 바구니에 타서 주변을 관람하는 동안, pilot은 원하는 direction으로 가기 위해 기낭의 공기와 대기의 layer를 적절히 이용하여 원하는 곳에 land할 수 있다고 해요. 자, 그럼 이제 열기구를 타고 하늘을 날아오르는 기분으로 열기구에 관해 좀 더 자세히 알아볼까요?

본문 미리보기 QUIZ

1 열기구에서 승객들이 탈 수 있는 곳은 [□ burner / □ basket] 이다. 34쪽에서 확인

2 열기구는 공기가 안정적인 저녁이나 [□ 이른 아침 / □ 점심때] 에 타는 것이 좋다. 36쪽에서 확인

독해의 장벽을 깨는 만만한 Vocabulary

Study Date: ____ / ____

□	1	**balloon** [bəlúːn]	명 기구, 풍선	열기구	a hot air ________
□	2	**book** [buk]	동 예약하다	비행을 예약하다	________ a flight
□	3	**direction** [dirékʃən]	명 방향	방향을 바꾸다	change ________
□	4	**fabric** [fǽbrik]	명 직물, 천	천 조각	a piece of ________
□	5	**flame** [fleim]	명 불꽃, 화염	큰 화염	a big ________
□	6	**float** [flout]	동 뜨다, 떠다니다	바다 위에 떠 있다	________ on the sea
□	7	**land** [lænd]	동 착륙하다	안전하게 착륙하다	________ safely
□	8	**layer** [léiər]	명 층	공기의 층	a ________ of air
□	9	**passenger** [pǽsəndʒər]	명 승객	승객용 좌석	the ________ seat
□	10	**pilot** [páilət]	명 조종사	비행기 조종사	an airplane ________
□	11	**principle** [prínsəpl]	명 원리, 원칙	과학적 원리	a scientific ________
□	12	**sink** [siŋk]	동 가라앉다	바닥까지 가라앉다	________ to the bottom
□	13	**still** [stil]	형 고요한, 정지한	바람 없는 고요한 공기	________ air
□	14	**temperature** [témpərətʃər]	명 온도	낮은 온도	a low ________
□	15	**unstable** [ʌnstéibl]	형 불안정한	불안정한 상태	________ conditions

어휘 자신만만 QUIZ

1 그것은 공기를 데우기 위해 큰 화염을 만들어 낸다.

It produces a big ____________ to heat the air.

2 낮 동안에는 온도가 상승한다.

During the day, the ____________ goes up.

Reading 01

Hot Air Balloon

My Reading Time | Words 173 / 2분 00초

1회 ____분____초 2회 ____분____초

What keeps a hot air balloon in the sky? The principle is simple: hot air rises, and cold air sinks. The hot air pushes the balloon up and keeps it floating.

A hot air balloon has three parts: the basket, the burner, and the envelope. The basket is the place where passengers ride. The burner is above the passengers' heads. It produces a big flame to heat the air. The envelope is the colorful fabric bag that holds the hot air. When the air inside the envelope is heated, the balloon rises.

Once in the air, the balloon just floats with the wind. The pilot does not know exactly where the balloon will land. However, he or she can control the landing by using different layers of air. The pilot can move the balloon up or down by controlling the heat in the envelope. Often the pilot can find a layer of air that will allow the balloon to change direction. On some days, the balloon may actually turn around in the air.

envelope

Words hot air balloon 열기구 principle 명 원리, 원칙 sink 동 가라앉다 float 동 뜨다, 떠다니다 envelope 명 기낭 passenger 명 승객 flame 명 불꽃, 화염 fabric 명 직물, 천 land 동 착륙하다 layer 명 층 allow 동 ~에게 허락하다 direction 명 방향 turn around 회전하다

LINK 실력 향상 WORKBOOK p.14

1

Title

본문의 다른 제목으로 가장 알맞은 것은?

a. How Does a Hot Air Balloon Fly?

b. Who Can Make a Hot Air Balloon?

c. How Many Layers of Air Are There?

d. When Is the Best Time to Fly a Hot Air Balloon?

2

Inference

버너를 끄면 일어날 일로 가장 알맞은 것은?

a. The basket will go up.

b. Passengers will feel safer.

c. The hot air balloon will fall.

d. The envelope will get bigger.

3

Details

본문의 내용과 일치하도록 알맞은 단어를 쓰시오.

Q: How can a pilot control the direction of a hot air balloon?

A: By flying in different _________ of air.

4

Summary

Complete the summary with the words in the box.

three	rises	envelope	landing	layers	two

A hot air balloon has _________ parts. The basket carries passengers, the burner heats the air, and the _________ holds the hot air. If we heat the air inside the envelope, the balloon _________. In the air, the pilot uses different _________ of air to control the _________.

지식백과

유명한 열기구 축제

앨버커키 국제 열기구 축제(Albuquerque International Balloon Fiesta)는 매년 10월 첫째 주에 미국 뉴멕시코 주의 앨버커키라는 도시에서 개최되며, 500개 이상의 열기구가 참여한다. 이곳의 10월 날씨는 온화하며, 바람의 방향을 정확히 예측할 수 있기 때문에 조종사들이 출발한 장소 가까이에 착륙하는 데 용이하다. 수백 개의 열기구가 한꺼번에 이륙할 수 있도록 행사는 300,000평방미터가 넘는 대평원에서 진행된다.

Reading 02

Enjoy Hot Air Ballooning

My Reading Time | Words 170 / 1분 55초

1회 ____분____초 2회 ____분____초

Hot air ballooning is probably the slowest way to fly, but it is one of the most exciting sports to enjoy. These days, many hot air balloon companies provide excellent, safe flying experiences. (A) There are a few tips for enjoying a hot air balloon ride, though.

Before booking a flight, first check out the company's safety record and the pilot's experience. (B) It is a good idea to ride a hot air balloon in the early morning or in the evening because the air is still at these times. (C) During the day, the temperature goes up. Since hot air rises, the balloon can be unstable. (D) Also, you need to remember it can be quite cold up in the sky. Warm clothes are strongly recommended.

Once in the air, you will glide silently across the sky. As you look down at all the busy people below, you may feel both excited and relaxed. Start saving for a hot air balloon ride now!

Words company 명 회사 excellent 형 뛰어난 book 동 예약하다 record 명 기록 still 형 고요한, 정지한 temperature 명 온도 unstable 형 불안정한 recommend 동 추천하다 glide 동 활공하다, (바람 따라) 공중을 미끄러지듯 나아가다

LINK 실력 향상 WORKBOOK p.16

Topic

1 What is the passage mainly about?

a. 열기구를 타기에 최적의 시간
b. 날씨가 열기구 안전에 미치는 영향
c. 열기구 탑승 예약을 쉽게 하는 방법
d. 안전하고 즐겁게 열기구를 타는 방법

Organization

2 주어진 문장이 들어가기에 가장 알맞은 곳은?

You can visit the company's website for all this information.

a. (A) b. (B) c. (C) d. (D)

Details

3 다음을 읽고 본문의 내용과 일치하면 T, 일치하지 않으면 F를 쓰시오.

(1) ______ The air is more stable in the morning than during the day.
(2) ______ The temperature in the air is often lower than on the ground.
(3) ______ When the air is still, it is dangerous to ride a hot air balloon.

Graphic Organizer

4 본문의 단어를 이용하여 표를 완성하시오.

Hot Air Ballooning

Company	Time	Clothes
a company with a good safety record and an experienced ________	early morning or evening when the air is ________	warm clothes as it is ________ up in the sky

지식백과

하늘에서 즐기는 스포츠

행글라이딩, 패러글라이딩 등 공중 유영을 즐기는 스포츠를 항공 스포츠라고 한다. 행글라이딩은 비행기처럼 생긴 무동력 장치(글라이더)를 타고 비행하는 스포츠인데, 탑승자는 벨트에 의지하여 글라이더에 매달린 상태에서 활강한다. 패러글라이딩은 낙하산 활강과 행글라이딩의 원리를 혼합한 스포츠이다. 동력 장치 없이 사람이 달려가면서 낙하산처럼 생긴 물체를 하늘로 날아오르게 하여 이륙을 하거나, 또는 제자리에서 이륙을 하여 비행을 한 후 두 발로 착륙을 한다.

비행기의 역사에 대해 동영상으로 알아보세요. Time 3' 50"

Reading Closer

독해의 내공을 키우는 마무리 학습

A Unit 04에서 학습한 단어를 생각해 보고, 다음 퍼즐을 완성해 보시오.

Across

❶ to move down to a lower position

❷ a person who operates hot air balloons or planes

❸ I cannot __________ your children.
(나는 네 아이들을 통제할 수 없다.)

❹ I thought that the plane could __________ safely.
(나는 그 비행기가 안전하게 착륙할 수 있을 것이라고 생각했다.)

❺ 느긋한, 여유 있는

Down

❶ not moving; quiet

❻ not stable; likely to change

❼ 기록; 음반

❽ the state of being free from danger

❾ a brightly burning gas from a fire

B 다음 [보기]에서 알맞은 말을 골라 문장을 완성하시오.

보기	float	passenger	allow	layer	fabric

1 The elderly woman was the only __________ on the bus.

2 This coat is not heavy because it is made of light __________.

3 The volcanic eruption covered the town with a thick __________ of ash.

4 Most parents do not __________ their young children to stay out late.

5 In the Dead Sea, anyone can easily __________ because it is very salty.

생각을 키우는 서술형 • 수행평가 대비 훈련

C 다음 네모 안에서 알맞은 말을 골라 글을 완성하시오.

The [principle / principal] of flying a hot air balloon has remained the same since it was first invented. Passengers ride in the [basket / envelope], and hot air from a fire lets the balloon [fall / rise] and fly in the air. Do you want to ride a balloon? Then [book / record] a flight with a company that has a good safety record. Wear warm clothes and enjoy the ride in the early morning when the air is [still / hot].

UNIT 05 In the Future

생각의 폭을 넓히는 **배경지식 Story**

#Topic Future Job

여러분은 미래에 어떤 직업을 갖고 싶은가요? 벌써 마음 속으로 later에 무엇이 되겠다고 decision을 한 친구도 있을 거예요.

직업의 종류는 무척 variety하답니다. 현재 우리나라에는 약 2만 개가 넘는 다양한 직종이 있다고 해요. 사람의 개성이 다양한 만큼 여러 직업이 있는 것이죠. 예를 들어, 하루 종일 라면을 먹어도 질리지 않고, 평생 라면만을 연구하는 데 regret하지 않는다면, 라면 개발자라는 직업도 좋을 것 같아요. 사진을 좋아하는 친구라면 photographer를, physics에 관심 있는 친구라면 과학자를, 미지의 세계를 explore하는 것을 좋아한다면 탐험가를 염두에 둬도 좋아요.

그런데 미래에는 어떠한 일이 생길지, 어떠한 직업들이 생기고 또 어떠한 직업들이 사라질지는 아무도 모른답니다. 백 년 전만해도 컴퓨터와 관련된 직업은 없었으니까요. 그래서 자신이 좋아하는 것이 무엇이고, 무엇을 잘할 수 있으며, 사회가 어떤 인재를 필요로 하는지, 자신이 어떠한 일을 할 수 있는지 끊임없이 조사하고 계획을 세워 실천해 나가는 노력이 필요한 거죠.

이번 시간에는, goal을 이루기 위해서 어떻게 해야 하는지를 보여 주는 이야기를 읽고 ideal한 직업 선택을 위해 keep in mind해야 할 중요한 조언들을 함께 읽어 봐요.

본문 미리보기 QUIZ

1 James Cameron은 [□ 터미널 / □ 터미네이터] 영화를 만들었다. 42쪽에서 확인

2 글쓴이는 직업 선택 시 기억해야 할 [□ 세 가지 / □ 네 가지]를 제시하고 있다. 44쪽에서 확인

독해의 장벽을 깨는 만만한 Vocabulary

Study Date: ____ / ____

☐	1	**college** [kálidʒ]	명 대학	대학교 학생	a ______ student
☐	2	**decision** [disíʒən]	명 결정, 결심	결정을 하다	make a ______
☐	3	**director** [diréktər]	명 감독	영화감독	a movie ______
☐	4	**explore** [iksplɔ́:r]	동 탐험하다	사막을 탐험하다	______ the desert
☐	5	**goal** [goul]	명 목표	내 인생의 목표	the ______ of my life
☐	6	**ideal** [aidí:əl]	형 이상적인	이상적인 세상	an ______ world
☐	7	**later** [léitər]	부 뒤에, 나중에	나중에	______ on
☐	8	**mind** [maind]	명 마음	명심하다	keep in ______
☐	9	**nightmare** [náitmὲər]	명 악몽	악몽을 꾸다	have a ______
☐	10	**photographer** [fətágrəfər]	명 사진작가	뉴스 사진기자	a news ______
☐	11	**physics** [fíziks]	명 물리학	물리학 실험	______ experiments
☐	12	**regret** [rigrét]	동 후회하다	그 결정을 후회하다	______ the decision
☐	13	**screenplay** [skrí:nplèi]	명 영화 대본, 시나리오	대본을 쓰다	write a ______
☐	14	**toward** [tɔ:rd]	전 ~쪽으로	강 쪽으로	______ the river
☐	15	**variety** [vəráiəti]	명 다양성	다양한, 가지가지의	a ______ of

어휘 자신만만 QUIZ

1 어느 날 그는 살인 로봇에 관한 악몽을 꿨다.

One day he had a ______ about a killer robot.

2 직업을 선택하는 것은 매우 중요한 결정이다.

Choosing a job is a very important ______.

Reading 01 Just One Dollar

My Reading Time | Words 156 / 1분 45초

1회 ____분 ____초 2회 ____분 ____초

Would you take a job if it paid just one dollar? Most people would not. What if it were your ideal job? Still, most people wouldn't go for it.

James Cameron, the movie director of *Avatar*, was different. In college, he studied physics and learned about special effects on his own. He always dreamed about becoming a movie director someday.

One day Cameron had a nightmare about a killer robot. The robot <u>send</u> from the future to kill him. The dream gave him the idea for *The Terminator*, and he wrote a screenplay for the movie in 1984. He badly wanted to direct his own movie. Many companies showed interest in the screenplay, but they wouldn't let Cameron direct it. Finally, Cameron found a company, Hemdale Pictures. They bought the screenplay for just one dollar and let him direct the movie. *The Terminator* was a box office hit, and Cameron made his dream come true.

Words

pay 동 지불하다　go for it 단호히 나아가다　movie director 영화감독　college 명 대학
physics 명 물리학　effect 명 효과　nightmare 명 악몽　terminator 명 종결시키는 사람
screenplay 명 영화 대본, 시나리오　come true 실현되다

LINK 실력 향상 WORKBOOK p.18

1 Title

본문의 다른 제목으로 가장 알맞은 것은?

a. Cameron's Favorite Movies

b. James Cameron's Ideal Job

c. The Hard Work of Movie Directors

d. Interesting Screenplays by Cameron

2 Grammar

밑줄 친 send의 알맞은 형태를 쓰시오

→ ____________________

3 Details

Cameron에 관한 설명 중 본문의 내용과 일치하는 것은?

a. 대학에서 감독 관련 교과목을 많이 이수했다.

b. 영화에 대한 영감은 주로 장난감 상점에서 얻었다.

c. 처음 감독한 영화는 「아바타」라는 작품이었다.

d. 「터미네이터」 시나리오를 1달러에 팔았다.

4 Graphic Organizer

본문의 단어를 이용하여 표를 완성하시오.

James Cameron

In college	After college	As a director
• studied ________ • learned about special ________ for himself	• wrote a ________ based on his dream • sold it to Hemdale Pictures for ________ dollar	• directed *The Terminator*, which was a box office ________ • also directed *Avatar*

지식백과

영화를 만드는 사람들

감독(director), 제작자(producer), 그리고 시나리오 작가(screenplay writer)는 영화를 만드는 데 없어서는 안 될 존재이다. 감독은 영화 제작 과정의 총 책임자에 해당하며, 특히 영화 장면들을 구상하고 촬영하는 데 핵심적인 역할을 한다. 제작자는 영화의 질을 높여 많은 관객을 끌 수 있도록 관리하며, 특히 영화를 만드는 데 소요되는 재정을 확보하는 역할을 맡는다. 시나리오 작가는 영화에 포함되는 이야기를 구상하고 등장인물들의 대사를 작성한다.

James Cameron이 시나리오를 1달러에 판 사연을 감상하세요. Time 12' 28"

Reading 02 Choosing a Job

My Reading Time | Words 174 / 2분 00초

1회 ____분____초 2회 ____분____초

How are you going to choose your ideal job? Choosing a job is a very important decision, so you should put some time and energy into it. There are three important things you should keep in mind when choosing a job.

5 First, remember that you are going to work (A) [round / around] 40 hours a week at your job. This means you will have to choose a job that you really like. If you like to spend the whole day cooking, you will be a good (B) [cook / cooker]. If you like to take photos, you might be a great photographer.

10 Second, explore the job of your choice. Gather information about the job from a variety of sources. You may even talk to someone who has your ideal job. This way, you can make a decision you won't regret later on.

Finally, write an action plan. You have to set goals to get the job you 15 want. Just thinking about an ideal job won't help you get it. You need to have clear goals and work toward them.

Words

decision 명 결정, 결심 keep in mind 명심하다 photographer 명 사진작가 explore 동 탐험하다 variety 명 다양성 ideal 형 이상적인 regret 동 후회하다 later on 나중에 action 명 행동 goal 명 목표 toward 전 ~쪽으로

LINK 실력 향상 WORKBOOK p.20

Topic

1 What is the passage mainly about?

a. how to set a clear goal
b. how to be a good cook
c. how to make decisions
d. how to find a perfect job

Words

2 (A)와 (B)에 들어갈 말로 바르게 짝지어진 것은?

	(A)		(B)
a.	round	……	cook
b.	round	……	cooker
c.	around	……	cook
d.	around	……	cooker

Details

3 필자가 권장하는 바가 아닌 것은?

a. Consider your interests when choosing a job.
b. Collect enough information about your ideal job.
c. Get some help from job counselors and your family.
d. Set up goals and try hard to achieve them.

Summary

4 Complete the summary with the words in the box.

ideal	like	dislike	goals	decisions	information

You should keep three things in mind when you choose a job. Consider what you __________ first. Second, collect __________ about the job from different sources. Finally, have clear __________ to get the job. They will help you get your __________ job.

지식백과

안전한 직업?

영국의 *The Guardian*은 미래 직업 세계를 예측하기는 어렵지만 자동화로 대체될 가능성이 높은 직업과 자동화로 대체하기 어려울 것으로 전망되는 직업을 제시하였다. 자동화로 대체될 가능성이 매우 높은 직업으로는 텔레마케터, 금전 출납원, 택시 운전기사, 패스트푸드 요리사 등을 꼽았고, 자동화로 대체하기 힘든 직업으로는 직업 치료사, 영양사, 의사, 종교인, 사회 복지사 등을 꼽았다. 하지만 미래를 정확히 예측하기란 불가능하기 때문에 전문가마다 다양한 의견이 제시되고 있다.

Reading Closer 독해의 내공을 키우는 마무리 학습

A Unit 05에서 학습한 단어를 생각해 보고, 다음 퍼즐을 완성해 보시오.

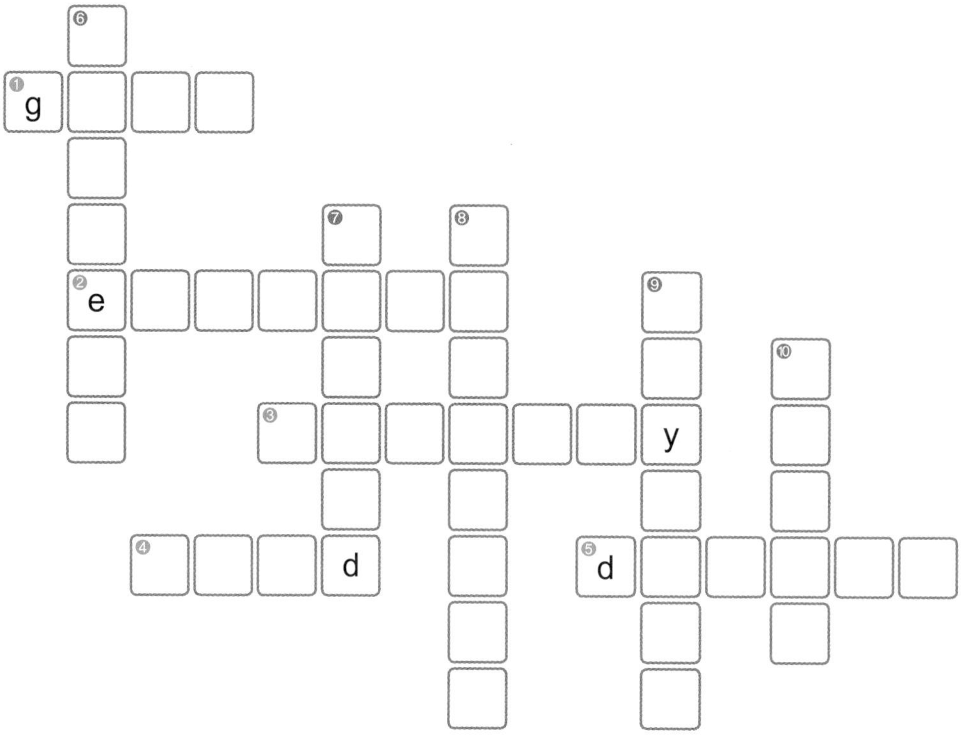

Across

❶ 목표를 세우다: set a __________

❷ to search or travel through a place for the purpose of discovery

❸ 다양한 형태와 색깔: a __________ of shapes and colors

❹ 명심하다: keep in __________

❺ The movie was __________ed by Steven Spielberg.

Down

❻ 대학생: a __________ student

❼ 강 쪽으로 움직이다: move __________ the river

❽ the act of making up your mind about something

❾ the science that deals with matter, energy, motion, and force

❿ 나중에: __________ on / 며칠 후에: a few days __________

B 다음 [보기]에서 알맞은 말을 골라 문장을 완성하시오.

보기	nightmare	ideal	gather	regret	effect

1 If you waste your time, you will __________ it later.

2 Parties are __________ opportunities to meet new people.

3 I read several books to __________ information about the topic.

4 My sister often has a __________ after she watches a horror movie.

5 I took some pills for the headache, but they did not have any __________.

생각을 키우는 서술형 • 수행평가 대비 훈련

C 다음 [보기]에서 알맞은 말을 골라 글을 완성하시오.

Choosing a job is an important __________, so you should do three things. First, make sure you choose a job that you really like. Second, __________ the job by gathering information about it from different __________. Finally, set a clear __________ and work hard to achieve it. James Cameron did all these. He liked the job of __________ movies, talked to different people about the job, and worked hard to make his dream come true.

보기	goal	decision	sources	directing	explore

생각의 폭을 넓히는 **배경지식 Story**

UNIT 06 Water for Life

#Topic Water Shortage

물은 우리 생활의 가장 essential한 것 중 하나이죠. 그런데 우리나라가 '물 부족 국가'라는 사실을 알고 있나요? 매일 샤워를 하거나 설거지나 청소 등의 household chores를 하더라도 물을 마음껏 쓸 수 있는데, 물 shortage 국가라니 incredible한 사실이 아닐 수 없어요. 하지만 국제 인구 행동 연구소는 우리나라를 주기적으로 물 shortage를 경험하는 나라로 분류해 놓고 있어요.

지구 표면의 3/4 이상을 덮고 있는 것이 물인데, 어째서 물이 부족하다고 말하는 것일까요? 그것은 대부분의 물이 우리가 마실 수 있는 깨끗한 상태가 아니거나 바닷물이기 때문이에요. 실제로 우리가 사용할 수 있는 물은 지구 전체의 물 중 약 0.3% 밖에 되지 않는다고 해요. 게다가 지속적인 인구 증가와 환경 오염, climate change 때문에 과학자들은 깨끗한 물의 supply가 앞으로 더 줄어들 것이라고 예측하고 있어요. 깨끗한 물이 decrease한다는 것은 곧 세계의 어떤 region에서는 더 많은 사람들이 risk에 처하게 된다는 것을 의미해요.

다행히도 세계의 많은 organization이 물 부족을 improve하기 위해 나서고 있고, 각 나라들도 물 문제 해결을 위해 서로의 경험과 knowledge를 공유하고 있어요. 하지만 근본적으로 우리와 같은 ordinary한 사람들부터 물을 아껴 쓰는 노력을 하지 않는다면, 물 문제 해결을 위한 어떠한 방법도 결국 소용이 없게 될 거예요.

본문 미리보기 QUIZ

1 Ryan Hreljac은 세계 여러 나라에 [□ 우물 / □ 집] 을 지었다. 50쪽에서 확인

2 중동과 [□ 남아프리카 / □ 북아프리카] 지역의 몇몇 국가들은 물이 충분하지 못하다. 52쪽에서 확인

독해의 장벽을 깨는 만만한 Vocabulary

Study Date: ______ / ______

☐ 1	**chore** [tʃɔːr]	명 잡일, 허드렛일	집안일, 가사 노동	household ________s
☐ 2	**climate** [kláimit]	명 기후	기후 변화	________ change
☐ 3	**decrease** [dikríːs]	동 감소하다	계속해서 감소하다	continue to ________
☐ 4	**essential** [isénʃəl]	형 필수적인	필수적인 요소	an ________ element
☐ 5	**foundation** [faundéiʃən]	명 재단	문화 재단	a cultural ________
☐ 6	**improve** [imprúːv]	동 개선하다	상황을 개선하다	________ the situation
☐ 7	**incredible** [inkrédəbl]	형 놀라운	놀라운 능력	an ________ ability
☐ 8	**knowledge** [nálidʒ]	명 지식	영어 지식	________ of English
☐ 9	**ordinary** [ɔ́ːrdənèri]	형 평범한, 보통의	평범한 사람들	________ people
☐ 10	**organization** [ɔ̀ːrgənizéiʃən]	명 조직, 기구	지역 조직	a local ________
☐ 11	**region** [ríːdʒən]	명 지방, 지역	물이 메마른 지역	a waterless ________
☐ 12	**risk** [risk]	명 위험	질병의 위험	the ________ of disease
☐ 13	**shortage** [ʃɔ́ːrtidʒ]	명 부족, 결핍	물 부족	water ________
☐ 14	**supply** [səplái]	명 공급	공급이 부족한	in short ________
☐ 15	**well** [wel]	명 우물	우물을 짓다	build a ________

어휘 자신만만 QUIZ

1 그는 넉 달 동안 온갖 종류의 집안일을 했다.

He did all kinds of household ________s for four months.

2 그것은 콜레라와 장티푸스와 같은 다양한 병의 위험성을 높인다.

It increases the ________ of various diseases like cholera and typhoid.

Reading 01

Ryan's Well

My Reading Time | Words 170 / 2분 00초

1회 ____분____초 2회 ____분____초

Ryan Hreljac learned from his teacher that many people in Africa were dying because they did not have enough clean water. (A) He wanted to do something about the problem. (B) He did all kinds of household chores for four months to raise his first $70. (C) With this money, his first well was built in 1999 in a village in Uganda. (D) Ryan was only seven years old.

Ryan has continued to raise money. He has given talks at hundreds of schools, churches, and events. People have felt sorry for those who are unable to drink clean water and have decided to give a helping hand. So far, Ryan's Well Foundation has built over 1,000 wells in more than a dozen countries.

When someone asks about his achievements, Ryan says he is just an ordinary person. As a young boy, he loved playing basketball, ice hockey, and video games. He graduated from college in 2013 and now works for the Ryan's Well Foundation. Ryan's success shows that ordinary people can do incredible things. Everyone is able to make the world a better place.

Words

well 명 우물　household chores 집안일, 가사 노동　continue 동 계속하다　raise money 돈을 모금하다　church 명 교회　be unable to ~을 할 수 없다　foundation 명 재단　achievement 명 성취　ordinary 형 평범한　graduate from ~을 졸업하다　success 명 성공　incredible 형 놀라운

LINK 실력 향상 WORKBOOK p.22

Main Idea

1 본문이 주는 교훈으로 가장 알맞은 것은?

a. 누구나 놀라운 일을 해 낼 수 있다.

b. 아프리카의 물 문제는 심각하다.

c. 비영리단체에 기부하는 것이 중요하다.

d. 정부가 수자원 확보에 투자해야 한다.

Organization

2 주어진 문장이 들어가기에 가장 알맞은 곳은?

He decided to raise money for building wells in Africa.

a. (A) b. (B) c. (C) d. (D)

Details

3 문장을 읽고 본문의 내용과 일치하면 T, 일치하지 않으면 F를 쓰시오.

(1) ______ Ryan's teacher explained the water problem in Africa.

(2) ______ The total amount of money that Ryan raised was $70.

(3) ______ Many people agreed to help Africans drink clean water.

Graphic Organizer

4 본문의 단어를 이용하여 표를 완성하시오.

Ryan's Well Foundation	
Start	• Many people in Africa didn't have enough __________ water. • Ryan built his first __________ in a village in Uganda.
Development	• People have decided to give a helping __________. • Ryan's Well Foundation has built over __________ wells so far.
Lesson	• Everyone can make the world a __________ place.

지식백과

우리나라의 물 사용

한 해 동안 우리나라에 유입되는 물의 양은 약 1,240억m^3이며, 이 중 42% 정도는 증발하고 나머지는 하천으로 흘러간다. 하천의 물 중에서도 절반 이상은 바다로 흘러 들어가기 때문에, 우리가 활용할 수 있는 물은 연간 337억m^3 정도에 불과하다고 한다. 이중 47% 정도는 농업용수로 사용되고, 23% 정도는 생활용수로 쓰이며, 나머지는 하천 유지와 공업용으로 이용된다.

Reading 02 The Right to Clean Water

My Reading Time | Words 159 / 1분 45초

1회 ____분 ____초 2회 ____분 ____초

Water is the most essential element for life. But in some countries in the Middle East and North Africa, many people don't have enough water. ________ climate change, the amount of water has decreased in this region.

Since clean water is in short supply, people sometimes have to drink unsafe water. It increases the risk of various diseases like *cholera and *typhoid. It also means they cannot bathe or clean their clothes properly. In many regions, girls have to walk many miles from their homes to get water instead of going to school.

To solve the problem, organizations like the World Bank started a project. The bank is helping several countries improve their water supply systems. The bank is also helping countries share their knowledge and experience. Water shortage is not just a problem in Africa or the Middle East. So the global community must work together to make sure that everyone has a right to clean water.

*cholera 콜레라 *typhoid 장티푸스

Words

essential 형 필수적인 element 명 요소 climate 명 기후 decrease 동 감소하다 region 명 지방, 지역 supply 명 공급 risk 명 위험 instead of ~ 대신에 organization 명 조직, 기구 improve 동 개선하다 knowledge 명 지식 shortage 명 부족, 결핍 community 명 공동체

LINK 실력 향상 WORKBOOK p.24

Topic

1 **What is the passage mainly about?**

a. the risk of various diseases

b. the importance of clean water

c. poverty in the Middle East and Africa

d. water shortage and efforts to solve the problem

Linking

2 **빈칸에 들어갈 말로 가장 알맞은 것은?**

a. Instead of

b. In spite of

c. Because of

d. In addition to

Details

3 **중동과 북아프리카의 상황에 대한 설명으로 본문의 내용과 일치하지 않는 것은?**

a. People don't have enough clean water.

b. Unsafe drinking water can cause many diseases.

c. They are trying to solve the problem by themselves.

d. The World Bank is helping improve the water supply systems.

Summary

4 **Complete the summary with the words in the box.**

wash	clean water	community	get water	go to school

Many people in the Middle East and North Africa don't have enough ______________. It is not easy to bathe or ___________ their clothes properly. Girls have to walk far away from their homes to ______________. To solve the problem, the global ___________ must work together.

지식 백과

세계 물의 날(World Water Day)

3월 22일은 세계 물의 날이다. 전 세계적으로 물 부족 현상이 심각하다는 점을 인식한 UN이 1992년 12월 총회의 결의에 따라 1993년에 처음 시작하였다. 이 날은 전 세계의 사람들이 물과 관련된 문제에 대해 인식하고 수자원의 보호를 위한 적절한 행동에 대해 생각해 볼 수 있는 기념일이다. UN은 매년 새로운 주제(theme)로 세계 물의 날을 기념하며, 많은 나라에서 다양한 행사가 개최된다.

아프리카의 물 부족 실태를 동영상으로 확인해 보세요. Time 4' 22"

Reading Closer

독해의 내공을 키우는 마무리 학습

A

Unit 06에서 학습한 단어를 생각해 보고, 다음 퍼즐을 완성해 보시오.

Across

❶ 충분한 음식: __________ food

❷ the average weather conditions of a certain region

❸ a place where you can keep your money in an account

❹ 공급과 수요: __________ and demand

❺ 믿을 수 없는 이야기: an __________ story

Down

❻ 우물을 파다: dig a __________

❼ She will __________ from middle school next year.
(그녀는 내년에 중학교를 졸업할 것이다.)

❽ the opposite of "increase"

❾ 지구 온난화: __________ warming

❿ 다양한 질병의 위험성: the __________ of various diseases

B

다음 [보기]에서 알맞은 말을 골라 문장을 완성하시오.

보기	ordinary	share	region	improve	shortage

1 Most farmers in this ________ grow grapes.

2 Best friends often ________ secrets with each other.

3 The hot dry summer has caused a serious water ________.

4 In spite of the operation, the patient's condition did not ________.

5 She is not a(n) ________ writer, but a very famous one.

생각을 키우는 서술형 • 수행평가 대비 훈련

C

다음 네모 안에서 알맞은 말을 골라 글을 완성하시오.

In some African countries, clean water is in short [supply / demand]. They have to walk a long distance to get clean water. They get various [regions / diseases] because of unsafe drinking water. Ryan Hreljac knew that water is [essential / incredible] for life, and that everyone has a [right / answer] to clean water. So, he decided to help build [homes / wells] in Africa. People have joined him and have built over 1,000 wells so far.

UNIT 07 In the Bathroom

생각의 폭을 넓히는 **배경지식 Story**

#Topic Flush Toilets

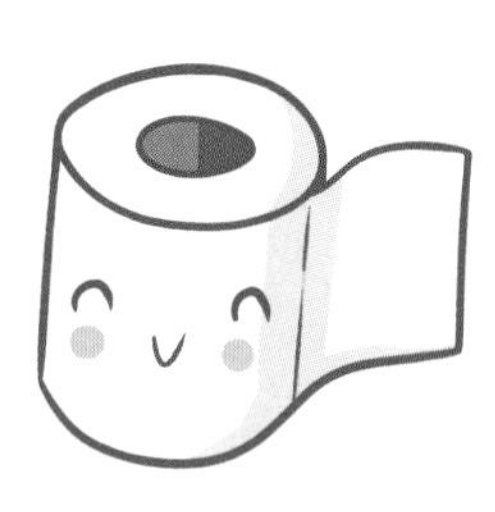

flush toilet은 ancient 문명에서도 발견될 정도로 오랜 역사를 자랑해요. 또한 로마인들은 잘 갖추어진 상하수도 시설과 함께 flush toilet을 사용했고요. 그러나 중세 유럽에서는 요강을 사용하거나 오물을 그냥 버렸다고 해요. 그래서 콜레라 같은 병균이 쉽게 spread되는 문제가 발생했죠.

오늘날과 유사한 수세식 화장실의 invention은 영국의 존 해링턴이 했어요. 1596년에, 그는 lever를 당기면 윗부분에 있는 물통에서 물이 흘러 내려와 배설물을 통으로 보내게 하는 수세식 화장실을 생각해 냈어요. 이는 사람들에게 엄청난 impact를 주었어요. 하지만 냄새가 여전하다는 단점이 있었죠. 그러다가 1775년에 영국의 알렉산더 커밍스가 배수 파이프를 중간에 U자 모양으로 구부러지게 하고 그 사이에 물을 채우게 했답니다. 그러자 파이프 밑에서부터 올라오던 냄새가 더 이상 나지 않게 되었어요. 그래서 지금도 화장실에 가면 구부러진 관을 볼 수 있답니다.

화장실에 가면 또 쉽게 볼 수 있는 것이 바로 화장지죠. ancient 그리스에서는 조약돌이나 clay를 사용해 뒤처리를 했다고 해요. 우리나라에서도 한 때 지푸라기나, 신문지 등을 사용했었는데 이제는 화장지로 replace되었지요. 이번 시간에는 우리가 깨끗하면서도 convenient한 삶을 누리게 해준 flush toilet와 toilet paper에 관해 알아보는 시간을 가져 보아요.

본문 미리보기 QUIZ

1 수세식 화장실은 [☐ 중력 / ☐ 원심력] 의 원리를 이용하여 작동된다. 58쪽에서 확인

2 화장지의 역사는 14세기 후반 [☐ 독일 / ☐ 중국] 까지 거슬러 올라간다. 60쪽에서 확인

독해의 장벽을 깨는 만만한 Vocabulary

Study Date: ____ / ____

☐ 1	**ancient** [éinʃənt]	형 고대의	고대의 그리스	________ Greece
☐ 2	**clay** [klei]	명 점토, 찰흙	점토 도자기	a ________ pot
☐ 3	**convenient** [kənvíːnjənt]	형 편리한	편리한 기능	________ functions
☐ 4	**efficient** [ifíʃənt]	형 효율적인	효율적인 체계	an ________ system
☐ 5	**gravity** [grǽvəti]	명 중력	중력의 당기는 힘	the pull of ________
☐ 6	**impact** [ímpækt]	명 충격, 영향	~에 영향을 주다	have an ________ on
☐ 7	**invention** [invénʃən]	명 발명, 발명품	놀라운 발명품	a wonderful ________
☐ 8	**lever** [lévər]	명 레버, 지레	레버를 당기다	pull the ________
☐ 9	**operation** [àpəréiʃən]	명 운용, 조작, 작동	기본적인 작동	the basic ________
☐ 10	**producer** [prədjúːsər]	명 제작자	영화 제작자	a film ________
☐ 11	**replace** [ripléis]	동 교체하다	배터리를 교체하다	________ the battery
☐ 12	**sensitive** [sénsətiv]	형 예민한, 민감한	민감한 피부	________ skin
☐ 13	**spread** [spred]	동 펴다, 퍼뜨리다	병을 퍼뜨리다	________ disease
☐ 14	**toilet** [tɔ́ilit]	명 변기, 화장실	수세식 화장실	a flush ________
☐ 15	**typical** [típikəl]	형 전형적인	전형적인 이야기	a ________ story

어휘 자신만만 QUIZ

1 질병은 옛날만큼이나 쉽게 전파될 수 없다.

Diseases cannot ____________ as easily as in the past.

2 화장지라는 아이디어가 그 당시에는 매우 민감한 것이었다.

The idea of toilet paper was too ____________ at that time.

Reading
01

How a Flush Toilet Works

My Reading Time | Words 176 / 2분 00초

1회 ____분____초 2회 ____분____초

These days, almost every house or building has flush toilets. Flush toilets have made our lives easier and cleaner. But they are not (A) a modern / an ancient invention. Flush toilets were first used in India about 2,700 years ago. There were also flush toilets in ancient Egypt, Persia, and China. While 5 the designs may vary, the basic operation is the same.

A flush toilet works because of gravity. A typical flush toilet has a water tank above its toilet bowl. When the lever is pulled, a plug in the tank opens. This allows water to flow out to fill the bowl. When the bowl is full enough, gravity causes the water to flow out through a pipe. The dirty 10 water goes out and is replaced by clean water.

The flush toilet allows us to live in much bigger cities. Because water cleans the toilets very well, diseases cannot spread as easily as in the past. The flush toilet may at first seem to be an invention of (B) major / minor importance, but its impact on our modern world is huge.

Words

flush toilet 수세식 화장실 invention 명 발명, 발명품 operation 명 운용, 조작, 작동 gravity 명 중력
typical 형 전형적인 lever 명 지레, 레버 pull 동 당기다 plug 명 마개 pipe 명 파이프, 관
replace 동 교체하다 major 형 주된 minor 형 사소한 impact 명 충격, 영향 huge 형 거대한

LINK 실력 향상 WORKBOOK p.26

Title

1 **각 단락과 제목을 연결하시오.**

(1) Paragraph 1 •
(2) Paragraph 2 •
(3) Paragraph 3 •

• The Effects of Flush Toilets
• The History of Flush Toilets
• The Way a Flush Toilet Works

Inference

2 **(A)와 (B)에 들어갈 말로 바르게 짝지어진 것은?**

	(A)		(B)
a.	a modern	……	major
b.	an ancient	……	major
c.	a modern	……	minor
d.	an ancient	……	minor

Details

3 **문장을 읽고 본문의 내용과 일치하면 T, 일치하지 않으면 F를 쓰시오.**

(1) ______ Flush toilets were invented recently.
(2) ______ Water is necessary for flush toilets to work.
(3) ______ Without gravity, flush toilets don't work.

Graphic Organizer

4 **본문의 단어를 이용하여 수세식 화장실의 작동 과정을 완성하시오.**

How a Flush Toilet Works

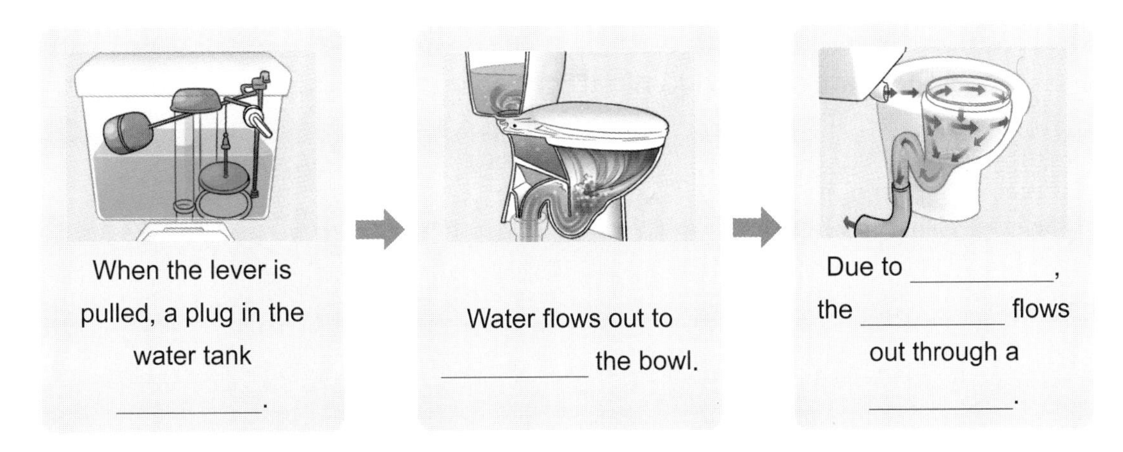

When the lever is pulled, a plug in the water tank __________.
Water flows out to __________ the bowl.
Due to __________, the __________ flows out through a __________.

지식백과

비행기 안 화장실

일반 가정의 수세식 화장실에서 배출된 오수는 주로 건물 지하에 설치된 정화조를 통해 처리된다. 반면에, 비행기 안의 화장실에서 발생하는 오수는 수거 방식으로 처리된다. 즉, 오수를 비행기 안에 모아 두었다가 비행기가 착륙하면 항공사에서 위탁한 업체가 오수를 수거해 가서 규정에 따라 처리한다. 이렇게 수거된 오수는 분뇨 처리장과 오수 처리장을 거쳐 먼 바다에 버려진다.

Reading 02

Toilet Paper

My Reading Time | Words 162 / 1분 50초

1회 ____분 ____초 2회 ____분 ____초

Have you ever wondered when toilet paper was invented? People in the past didn't use toilet paper. Instead of toilet paper, people used everything you can imagine—wood, leaves, water, or snow. The ancient Greeks used stones and pieces of clay. People in the Middle East commonly used the left hand. So, that hand is still considered unclean in that part of the world.

(A) The history of toilet paper goes back to the late 14th century in China. (B) Chinese emperors used a large sheet of paper which was specially produced. (C) Rolled toilet paper was invented around 1880. (D) The Scott Paper Company was the first producer of modern toilet paper. But the company didn't put its name on the product. The idea of toilet paper was too embarrassing and sensitive at that time.

Today there are over 5,000 different companies producing toilet paper around the world. Their products make our lives more convenient, efficient, and cleaner.

Words wonder 동 궁금해하다 invent 동 발명하다 imagine 동 상상하다 clay 명 점토, 찰흙 consider 동 고려하다, 간주하다 emperor 명 황제 expensive 형 비싼 producer 명 생산자 embarrassing 형 당황스러운 sensitive 형 예민한, 민감한 convenient 형 편리한 efficient 형 효율적인

Study Date: /

LINK 실력 향상 WORKBOOK p.28

Topic

1 What is the passage mainly about?

a. the ancient toilet systems

b. the history of toilet paper

c. toilets in the Middle East

d. the first producer of toilet paper

Organization

2 주어진 문장이 들어가기에 가장 알맞은 곳은?

But only emperors could use this expensive paper.

a. (A) b. (B) c. (C) d. (D)

Details

3 화장지에 관한 설명 중 본문의 내용과 일치하는 것은?

a. It was first used in ancient Greece.

b. In the 14th century, it was widely used in China.

c. The Scott Paper Company named their first toilet paper Scott.

d. There are about five thousand toilet paper companies these days.

Summary

4 Complete the summary with the words in the box.

China	cleaner	rolled	Greece	emperors	expensive

The first toilet paper was invented in the late 14th century in __________. But this was only for __________. The Scott Paper Company first produced __________ toilet paper. Today many companies are producing toilet paper. It makes our lives more convenient, efficient, and __________.

지식 백과

화장지와 문화 충격

서양에서는 화장지가 화장실에서만 사용된다. 하지만 한국에서는 화장지를 식탁에서 냅킨 대신 사용하는 경우가 있다. 적지 않은 외국인들은 이를 보고 문화 충격(culture shock)을 느끼기도 한다. 그렇기 때문에 전 세계에서 관광객이 몰려드는 제주도는 2006년 "제주특별자치도 식품접객업 운영기준에 관한 조례"를 제정하여 섬 내의 식당에서 화장지를 식탁에 올려놓을 경우에 벌금을 부과하고 있다.

옛날 사람들은 어떻게 볼일을 봤는지 동영상으로 확인해 보세요. Time 2' 19"

A Unit 07에서 학습한 단어를 생각해 보고, 다음 퍼즐을 완성해 보시오.

Across

❶ 중국의 마지막 황제: the last ________ of China

❷ I think she is too ________ about her age.
(그녀는 나이에 너무 민감한 것 같다.)

❸ the opposite of “major”

❹ 전형적인 경우: a ________ case

Down

❺ to be different or to become different: change

❻ 중력의 힘: the force of ________

❼ the opposite of “ancient”

❽ 변기의 물을 내리다: flush the ________

❾ to place things over a large area; to move into more places

❿ The bowl was made with ________.
(그 그릇은 점토로 만들어졌다.)

B 다음 [보기]에서 알맞은 말을 골라 문장을 완성하시오.

보기 embarrassing efficient replace invention impact

1 The campaign had a strong ________ on young people.

2 Robots will probably ________ most workers in the factory.

3 Thomas Edison is well-known for his ________ of the light bulb.

4 Bicycles provide a cheap and ________ way to travel downtown.

5 "How much money do you make?" can be an ________ question.

생각을 키우는 서술형 • 수행평가 대비 훈련

C 다음 [보기]에서 알맞은 말을 골라 글을 완성하시오.

There were flush toilets in ________ times. Today, almost every house or building has flush toilets. While the designs may ________, the operation is the same. Flush toilets, together with ________ toilet paper, can make our lives more ________. They also help us live in a healthier way because water cleans the toilets very well and diseases cannot ________ easily.

보기 spread convenient modern ancient vary

UNIT 08 Environment

생각의 폭을 넓히는 배경지식 Story

#Topic New Energy & Carbon Footprint

Energy released back into space
Reflected sunlight
Sunlight
Greenhouses gases (trap heat)
CO_2 CF_6 NO_2 CH_4
Energy absorbed

석탄과 석유를 왜 화석 연료라고 할까요? 그것은 오래전에 식물이나 동물이 땅에 묻혀서 화석처럼 높은 압력을 받아 생긴 것이기 때문이에요. 그런데 화석 연료를 태우면 공기 중으로 많은 carbon dioxide가 emission되고, 이 이산화탄소가 지구의 열을 trap하기 때문에 지구는 온실처럼 뜨거워지게 되어요. 이는 심각한 greenhouse 효과를 불러 일으켜요. 그래서 세계 여러 나라에서는 환경을 destroy하는 화석 연료를 대체할 수 있는 에너지를 연구하고 있답니다.

최근에는 바이오 에너지가 화석 연료를 대신할 새로운 에너지로 주목 받고 있어요. 바이오 에너지는 sunlight을 사용하여 광합성을 하는 유기물의 에너지를 사용하여 대체 에너지원을 만드는 것이에요. 그 중에서도 바이오 fuel이란 우리가 흔히 보는 사탕수수, 감자, 곡물, 식물성 기름, 해조류, 가축의 분뇨 등으로부터 얻을 수 있는 친환경 연료예요. 그래서 땅콩이나 콩의 기름으로 자동차를 달리게 할 수도 있답니다.

바이오 에너지뿐 아니라 solar energy, 풍력, 지열 에너지 등 다양한 대체 에너지에 대한 연구가 계속 되고 있어요. 하지만 이러한 노력과 함께 우리는 실생활에서 온실 가스를 줄이기 위한 노력이 필요해요. carbon footprint는 우리가 일상생활에서 얼마나 많은 탄소를 만들어 내는지를 measure하여 양으로 표시한 것이에요. 자동차를 이용하는 것보다는 대중교통을, 대중교통보다는 자전거나 직접 걷는 것이 탄소 발자국을 줄이는 길이랍니다.

본문 미리보기 QUIZ

1 Ms. Green은 [□ 태양열 / □ 전기] 에너지를 이용하여 요리를 하였다. 66쪽에서 확인

2 탄소 발자국과 관련 있는 것은 [□ CO_2 / □ H_2O] 이다. 68쪽에서 확인

독해의 장벽을 깨는 만만한 Vocabulary

Study Date: ______ / ______

☐ 1	**carbon** [kɑ́ːrbən]	명 탄소	이산화탄소	________ dioxide
☐ 2	**destroy** [distrɔ́i]	동 파괴하다	도시를 파괴하다	________ the city
☐ 3	**electricity** [ilektrísəti]	명 전기	전기를 절약하다	save ________
☐ 4	**emission** [imíʃən]	명 배출, 방출	열의 방출	________ of heat
☐ 5	**escape** [iskéip]	동 탈출하다	탈출하려고 시도하다	try to ________
☐ 6	**footprint** [fútprìnt]	명 발자국	발자국을 남기다	leave a ________
☐ 7	**fuel** [fjúːəl]	명 연료	연료를 태우다	burn ________
☐ 8	**greenhouse** [gríːnhàus]	명 온실	온실 효과	a ________ effect
☐ 9	**maintain** [meintéin]	동 유지하다	가격을 유지하다	________ the price
☐ 10	**measure** [méʒər]	동 측정하다	시간을 측정하다	________ the time
☐ 11	**reflective** [rifléktiv]	형 반사하는	반사광	________ light
☐ 12	**solar** [sóulər]	형 태양의	태양열 에너지	________ energy
☐ 13	**sunlight** [sʌ́nlàit]	명 햇빛	강한 햇빛	strong ________
☐ 14	**trap** [træp]	동 ~을 잡다, 가두다	에너지를 가두다	________ energy
☐ 15	**vegetable** [védʒətəbl]	명 채소	채소 재배	________ gardening

어휘 자신만만 QUIZ

1 반사하는 금속이 더 많은 햇빛을 가두는 데 사용된다.

The reflective metal is used to ____________ more sunlight.

2 그것은 연료를 태워서 나오는 이산화탄소 배출량을 측정한다.

It measures the carbon dioxide ____________s from burning fuels.

Reading 01 Cook with the Sun

My Reading Time | Words 170 / 1분 55초

1회 ____분____초 2회 ____분____초

It is a cool, but sunny day. Ms. Green is ready to cook her dinner. She opens the door of her home and goes outside. She gets everything ready in a pot. Then she goes to a park to play with her children. When she comes back, dinner will be waiting for her.

5 On sunny days, she doesn't cook in the kitchen. She cooks outside with solar energy. The principle of solar cooking is simple. She puts a dark pot in a sunny place. The pot takes in sunlight. The sunlight changes into heat. A mirror or reflective metal is used to trap more sunlight. A glass cover then prevents heat inside the pot from escaping.

10 How hot will the pot get? It depends, but with enough sunlight, the pot can reach 150 degrees Celsius. She can cook vegetables, rice, fish, and even meat. She doesn't need to use any electricity or gas to cook her food. She doesn't have to heat 15 up the house on hot summer days, either.

Words

pot 명 냄비, 솥 solar 형 태양의 principle 명 원리 sunlight 명 햇빛 reflective 형 반사하는 trap 동 ~을 잡다, 가두다 prevent 동 ~을 막다 escape 동 탈출하다 degree 명 도(度), 정도 Celsius 형 섭씨의 vegetable 명 채소 electricity 명 전기

Study Date: ____ / ____

LINK 실력 향상 WORKBOOK p.30

1 Title

본문의 단락 순서대로 알맞은 제목을 찾아 번호를 쓰시오.

- ☐ Advantages of Solar Cooking
- ☐ The Principle of Solar Cooking
- ☐ Ms. Green's Special Way of Cooking

2 Details

태양열을 이용한 요리에 필요하지 않은 것은?

a. a black pot
b. hot water
c. a reflective metal
d. a glass cover

3 Inference

태양열을 이용한 요리의 장점으로 가장 알맞은 것은?

a. You can cook outside anytime.
b. You can prepare food very quickly.
c. You don't have to use gas to cook.
d. You don't need any cooking device.

4 Summary

Complete the summary with the words in the box.

glass	cover	electricity	solar	dark pot	heat

Ms. Green has a special way to cook. She cooks outside on sunny days. She puts food in a ____________ and cooks with __________ energy. The pot takes in sunlight, and then the sunlight changes into __________. With solar cooking, Ms. Green doesn't need any __________ or gas.

지식백과

태양광과 태양열의 차이

태양 에너지는 풍력과 함께 가장 널리 알려진 재생 에너지이다. 태양 에너지는 주로 태양광 발전과 태양열 발전에 이용된다. 전자의 경우, 집광 판에 빛이 모이면 반도체의 특정 인자가 태양의 '빛'에 반응하여 전기를 만들게 된다. 후자의 경우, 태양의 '열'을 이용하여 물을 데우고 뜨거운 물이 수증기로 변하면 그 수증기를 이용하여 터빈을 돌려서 전기를 생산한다.

Reading 02

Carbon Footprint

My Reading Time | Words 169 / 1분 55초

1회 ____분 ____초 2회 ____분 ____초

Every single thing you buy at a supermarket creates greenhouse gases. For example, a paper cup weighs only 5 grams, but it produces 11 grams of greenhouse gases. A *kiwifruit creates greenhouse gases five times its own weight to get to your country from New Zealand. To measure the amount of greenhouse gases created by a product, people use the term "carbon footprint."

The carbon footprint shows how much greenhouse gases a product creates. It is the sum of two parts, the primary footprint and the secondary footprint. The primary footprint measures the direct CO_2 emissions from burning fuels for production and transportation. The secondary footprint measures the indirect CO_2 emissions from the whole life cycle of a product. CO_2 emissions are created not only from making products but also from maintaining and destroying them.

Now you know how much greenhouse gases a product can create. The next step is to choose products that cause less CO_2 emissions. By shopping more carefully, you can help save the planet.

*kiwifruit 키위, 참다래

Words

create 동 만들어 내다 greenhouse gas 온실가스 weigh 동 무게가 ~이다 measure 동 측정하다 carbon 명 탄소 footprint 명 발자국 primary 형 주요한, 최초의 secondary 형 제2의 emission 명 배출, 배출량 not only A but also B A뿐만 아니라 B도 maintain 동 유지하다 destroy 동 파괴하다

Study Date: ______ / ______

LINK 실력 향상 WORKBOOK p.32

1 Main Idea

What is the main idea of the passage?

a. 외국에서 수입한 과일은 많은 온실가스를 만들어 낸다.

b. 탄소 발자국이란 개념이 지구를 살리는 데 도움이 된다.

c. 제품 생산과 소비의 전 과정을 통해 온실가스가 배출된다.

d. 탄소 발자국은 일차 및 이차 탄소 발자국의 합이다.

2 Inference

문장의 빈칸에 알맞은 숫자를 쓰시오.

According to the passage, 40 grams of kiwifruit from New Zealand produces __________ grams of greenhouse gases.

3 Details

문장을 읽고 본문의 내용과 일치하면 T, 일치하지 않으면 F를 쓰시오.

(1) _____ A paper cup creates greenhouse gases about twice its weight.

(2) _____ The primary footprint refers to greenhouse gases from important products.

(3) _____ Greenhouse gases are also created when we destroy products.

4 Graphic Organizer

본문의 단어를 이용하여 표를 완성하시오.

Carbon footprint		The primary footprint		The __________ footprint
the amount of __________ gases created by a product	=	the direct CO_2 emissions from burning __________	+	the indirect CO_2 emissions from the whole life cycle of a product

또 다른 환경 지표, 물 발자국(water footprint)

물 발자국은 탄소 발자국(carbon footprint)과 마찬가지로 인간의 활동이 환경에 미치는 영향을 나타내는 지표 중 하나이다. 구체적으로, 물 발자국은 제품이나 서비스 생산 전 과정을 거쳐서 직접적으로 혹은 간접적으로 사용되는 물의 총량을 뜻하며, 일상생활에서 우리가 사용하는 제품과 서비스를 생산하고 소비하는 데 얼마나 많은 양의 물이 필요한지를 나타낸다. 참고로, 달걀 1개와 닭고기 1kg의 물 발자국은 각각 200리터와 3,900리터이다.

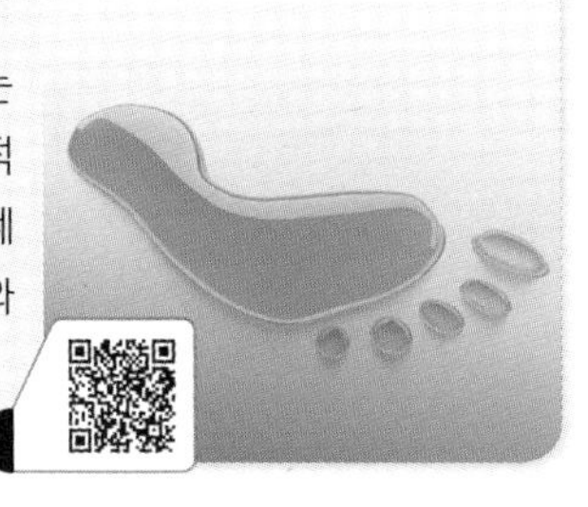

물 발자국에 대해 동영상으로 좀 더 알아보세요. Time 4' 21"

A Unit 08에서 학습한 단어를 생각해 보고, 다음 퍼즐을 완성해 보시오.

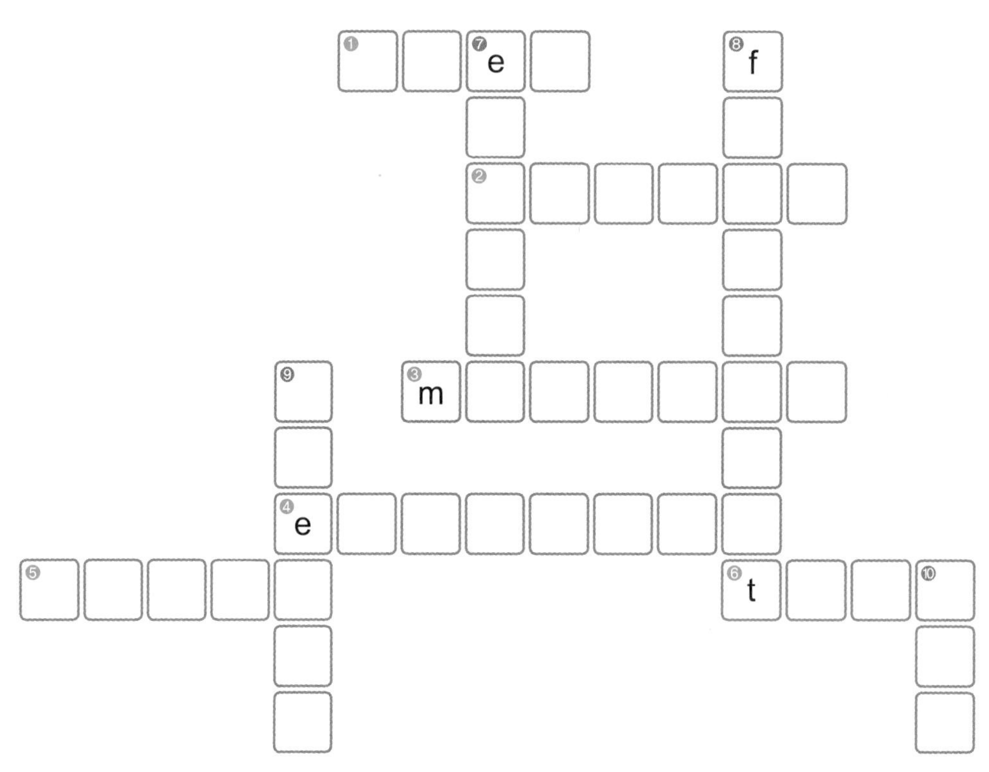

Across

❶ a material that is burned to produce heat or power

❷ 이산화탄소: __________ dioxide

❸ 각도를 재다: __________ the angle

❹ the act of producing or sending out something such as gas

❺ 태양열 에너지: __________ energy

❻ 가두다

Down

❼ to get away from a place such as a prison

❽ a track or mark left by a foot or shoe

❾ __________ is the ability and strength to do active physical things.

❿ A __________ is a deep round container used for cooking food.

B 다음 [보기]에서 알맞은 말을 골라 문장을 완성하시오.

보기	primary	weight	prevent	transportation	principle

1 It is important to ________ accidents on the road.

2 Seoul has an excellent network of public ________.

3 The ________ goal of the project is to raise enough money.

4 After two weeks of dieting, there was a decrease in his ________.

5 The most important ________ is that everyone is equal before the law.

생각을 키우는 서술형 • 수행평가 대비 훈련

C 다음 네모 안에서 알맞은 말을 골라 글을 완성하시오.

The carbon footprint shows how much greenhouse gases a product will [create / measure]. It includes greenhouse gases not only from burning [products / fuels] for production and [transportation / emission], but also from maintaining and destroying products. One way to save the [planet / plant] from greenhouse gases is by using solar energy. If we use it instead of fuels when we cook, for example, we will [measure / cause] less greenhouse gas emissions.

UNIT 09 Traveling Thailand

생각의 폭을 넓히는 배경지식 Story

#Topic Thailand

Thailand는 한국 전쟁 때 우리를 돕기 위해 especially 군대까지 파견해 준 고마운 나라예요. 태국은 헌법에 따라 왕이 통치하는 입헌 군주제 국가이며, 국민 대부분은 불교를 믿는다고 해요. 그래서 태국에는 관광지마다 temple이 많아요. 태국은 특히 세계적인 주요 쌀 수출국이라 할 수 있는데, 쌀과 관련된 재미있는 신화가 있어요.

아주 오랜 옛날, 태국에서는 상아사 할아버지와 상아시 할머니가 살았어요. 할아버지는 무서운 짐승이 지키고 있는 faraway한 jungle에서 거인이 무엇인가를 재배하고 있는 것을 알았어요. 그는 bravely하게 사람을 보내 제발 나눠달라고 간청했고, 거인은 남자 어른의 팔뚝만한 씨앗을 하나 주었어요. 할아버지는 relief하고, 이것을 진흙탕에 심자, 곧 싹이 돋아나 자라 벼가 되었다고 해요. 태국에서 쌀은 이처럼 오랜 신화를 가진 소중한 존재라고 할 수 있어요.

중국 명나라 때의 「서유기」라는 작품에는 손오공이라는 아주 뛰어난 능력을 가진 monkey가 나와요. 그런데 이 손오공의 모델이 바로 원숭이 임금님인 하누만이라는 이야기가 있어요. 예로부터 인도와 태국 등의 동남아 국가에서는 하늘을 날고 바다를 뛰어넘는 초능력을 지닌 원숭이 hero 하누만에 관한 legend가 널리 퍼져 있었거든요. 자, 이제 이야기를 통해서 legend의 내용을 좀 더 자세히 알아볼까요?

본문 미리보기 QUIZ

1 태국 사람들은 원숭이가 [□ 재앙을 / □ 행운을] 가져온다고 생각한다. 74쪽에서 확인

2 글쓴이가 태국에서 경험한 것은 [□ 코끼리 타기 / □ 코끼리 목욕시키기] 이다. 76쪽에서 확인

독해의 장벽을 깨는 만만한 Vocabulary

Study Date: ______ / ______

□ 1	**bravely** [bréivli]	부 용감하게	용감하게 싸우다	fight ________
□ 2	**demon** [dí:mən]	명 악마	악마가 되다	become a ________
□ 3	**especially** [ispéʃəli]	부 특별히	특별히 바쁘다	be ________ busy
□ 4	**faraway** [fá:rəwèi]	형 먼, 멀리의	먼 나라	a ________ country
□ 5	**forest** [fɔ́:rist]	명 숲	숲 속에서	in the ________
□ 6	**hero** [híərou]	명 영웅	전쟁 영웅	a war ________
□ 7	**jungle** [dʒʌ́ŋgl]	명 정글, 밀림 습지	정글의 법칙	law of the ________
□ 8	**kingdom** [kíŋdəm]	명 왕국	동물의 왕국	animal ________
□ 9	**legend** [lédʒənd]	명 전설	아더 왕의 전설	________ of King Arthur
□ 10	**relief** [rilí:f]	명 안심, 안도	큰 안도감	a great ________
□ 11	**rescue** [réskju:]	동 구하다, 구조하다	아기를 구하다	________ a baby
□ 12	**scenery** [sí:nəri]	명 풍경, 경치	아름다운 풍경	beautiful ________
□ 13	**shout** [ʃaut]	동 외치다	그에게 외치다	________ at him
□ 14	**sway** [swei]	동 흔들리다	바람에 흔들리다	________ in the wind
□ 15	**temple** [témpl]	명 사원, 신전	고대의 사원	the ancient ________

어휘 자신만만 QUIZ

1 그 원숭이는 Sita를 구하기 위해 용감하게 싸웠다.

The monkey fought bravely to ____________ Sita.

2 나는 안도의 큰 한숨을 내쉬었다.

A huge sigh of ____________ came out of me.

Reading 01 The Legend of Hanuman

My Reading Time | Words 161 / 1분 50초

1회 ____분 ____초 2회 ____분 ____초

In Thailand, monkeys are special animals. People are especially kind to monkeys in temples. Every day people bring food for the monkeys. They think it will bring them good luck. Why are monkeys so special in Thailand? There is a legend that explains why.

5 Once upon a time, the god Rama and his wife Sita lived in the forest. They were happy together. One day a demon came from a faraway land and took Sita to his kingdom. Sita was beautiful, so the demon wanted to marry her.

Rama and his brother searched 10 for Sita everywhere, but they could not find her. Luckily, they met a flying monkey whose name was Hanuman. He was clever and strong. He wanted to help Rama. 15 Soon Hanuman found out that the demon had taken Sita to the Island of Lanka. The monkey fought bravely to rescue Sita. Finally, Hanuman helped Rama save his wife Sita. Because of this, Hanuman became a hero across Thailand.

Words

especially 부 특별히 temple 명 사원 legend 명 전설 once upon a time 옛날에 forest 명 숲 demon 명 악마 faraway 형 먼, 멀리의 kingdom 명 왕국 search 동 찾다 bravely 부 용감하게 rescue 동 구하다, 구조하다 hero 명 영웅 across 전 ~의 전역에

LINK 실력 향상 WORKBOOK p.34

1

Main Idea

What is the main idea of the passage?

a. Rama fought against a demon with Hanuman.

b. People always give food to monkeys in Thailand.

c. A demon wanted to marry Sita and took her to his kingdom.

d. Monkeys are special in Thailand because a monkey helped Rama.

2

Details

본문의 내용으로 보아, 빈칸에 들어갈 말로 가장 알맞은 것은?

People in Thailand believed that __________ brings good luck.

a. living in the forest

b. talking about a legend

c. going to see monkeys

d. giving food to monkeys

3

Details

다음 중 본문의 내용과 일치하지 않는 것은?

a. Rama와 Sita는 숲 속에서 살았다.

b. 악마가 결혼하려고 Sita를 데려갔다.

c. Hanuman은 Sita가 어디에 있는지 알아냈다.

d. Rama의 형제가 Sita를 랑카 섬으로 데리고 갔다.

4

Graphic Organizer

본문의 단어를 이용하여 인물 간의 관계를 나타내는 표를 완성하시오.

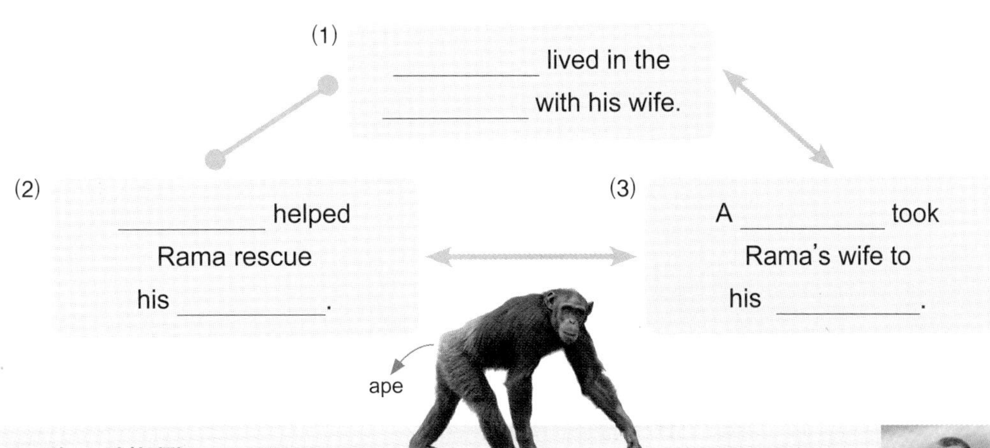

(1) __________ lived in the __________ with his wife.
(2) __________ helped Rama rescue his __________.
(3) A __________ took Rama's wife to his __________.
ape

지식 백과

monkey와 ape의 차이점

우리말에서는 monkey와 ape 둘 다 '원숭이'로 불리며, 인간과 같이 영장류(primate)로 분류된다. 그렇다면 monkey와 ape의 차이점은 무엇일까? 우선, 대부분의 monkey는 꼬리를 가지고 있으며, 상대적으로 체구가 작고, 네 발로 걸으며, 도구를 사용하지 않는다. 반면에, ape는 꼬리를 가지고 있지 않으며, 상대적으로 체구가 크고, 두 발로 걸을 수 있으며, 도구를 사용할 수 있다.

Reading 02

On the Elephant's Back

My Reading Time | Words 173 / 2분 00초

1회 ____분 ____초 2회 ____분 ____초

Last week, my family spent our holidays in Thailand. I enjoyed the food and beautiful scenery. I also enjoyed *whitewater rafting and hiking in the jungle. But there was one thing I couldn't enjoy. It was riding an elephant!

On a bright morning, I stood directly beside one of these huge animals for the first time in my life. I had to climb up an ancient ladder to get up to the elephant's back. With fear in my heart, I slowly sat down on the seat on its back. When the driver shouted into the elephant's ear, the elephant suddenly moved forward. The elephant was just walking, but I felt like it was moving very quickly. I swayed from side to side. For the next several minutes, I put all my strength into holding the handle on the seat.

After walking through the forest, we finally stopped. A huge sigh of relief came out of me. I was almost in tears. The driver asked, "Do you want one more round?" I screamed, "NOOOO!"

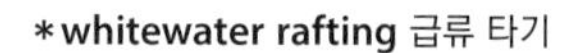

*whitewater rafting 급류 타기

Words

elephant 명 코끼리 holiday 명 휴가, 공휴일 scenery 명 풍경, 경치 jungle 명 정글, 밀림 습지
beside 전 …의 옆에 climb 동 오르다 ladder 명 사다리 shout 동 외치다 sway 동 흔들리다
from side to side 좌우로 strength 명 힘 relief 명 안심, 안도 sigh 명 한숨

Study Date: ______ / ______

LINK 실력 향상 WORKBOOK p.36

1 Topic

본문의 주제로 가장 알맞은 것은?

a. the scenery in Thailand

b. how to ride an elephant safely

c. the popularity of riding elephants

d. an experience of riding an elephant

2 Reference

밑줄 친 these huge animals가 가리키는 것을 영어로 쓰시오.

→ ______________________

3 Feelings

코끼리를 타기 전과 후에 느낀 필자의 감정 변화를 가장 잘 나타낸 것은?

a. worried → angry

b. afraid → relieved

c. fearful → nervous

d. excited → sad

4 Summary

Complete the summary with the words in the box.

handle	nice	ladder	stopped	terrible	started

I enjoyed my holidays in Thailand, but riding an elephant was a __________ experience. I climbed up a __________ and sat on the elephant's back. When the elephant started to walk, I was so afraid. I held the __________ on the seat very tightly. When we finally __________, I was relieved. I didn't want to ride it again.

지식 백과

태국의 상징: 코끼리

코끼리는 태국을 상징하는 동물로서 1855년부터 1916년까지 태국의 국기에는 빨간색 바탕에 흰 코끼리가 그려져 있었다. 태국에서는 1500년대 후반에 외부의 적으로부터 왕국을 보호하기 위해 체구가 크고 힘이 센 코끼리를 이용했다고 한다. 오랫동안 코끼리는 태국의 정글에서 무거운 목재 등을 운반하는 데에도 활용되었다. 코끼리는 대략 10살이 될 때까지 훈련을 받은 후 일에 투입되었으며, 60살 정도가 되면 은퇴하였다.

태국에서 코끼리의 의미에 관해 동영상으로 알아보세요. Time 2' 32"

Reading Closer

독해의 내공을 키우는 마무리 학습

A

Unit 09에서 학습한 단어를 생각해 보고, 다음 퍼즐을 완성해 보시오.

⑥ t

① _ _ _ k _ _

② _ _ _ _ e _

⑧ f

⑩ s

Across

❶ Hanuman is a flying __________. (Hanuman은 날아다니는 원숭이다.)

❷ 안도의 큰 한숨: a huge sigh of __________

❸ to save someone or something from danger

❹ The lion is the king of the __________. (사자는 밀림의 왕이다.)

Down

❺ 코끼리의 등 위에서: on the elephant's __________

❻ 절, 사찰, 사원

❼ a story from the past that is believed by many people but cannot be proved to be true

❽ a large piece of land covered with trees

❾ You will become a __________ one day. (너는 언젠가는 영웅이 될 것이다.)

❿ 흔들리다 (to move slowly back and forth)

Study Date: _____ / _____

B 다음 [보기]에서 알맞은 말을 골라 문장을 완성하시오.

보기	temple	search	ladder	relief	rescue

1 Bulguksa is a _________ in the capital of the Shilla Kingdom.

2 The man shouted for help, but nobody came to _________ him.

3 Everyone had a sense of _________ after the math exam.

4 The boy was standing on the _________ to clean the windows.

5 The police will _________ for the missing girl when the sun comes up.

생각을 키우는 서술형 • 수행평가 대비 훈련

C 다음 [보기]에서 알맞은 말을 골라 글을 완성하시오.

Riding on an elephant's back is scary but wonderful. On the elephant's back, you may _________ from side to side, but you can enjoy the beautiful _________ in Thailand. You can also breathe in fresh air as the _________ animal takes you through the jungle slowly. If the driver tells you about the _________ of Hanuman, you will learn about why monkeys are so _________ in Thailand.

보기	special	sway	huge	legend	scenery

UNIT 10 Thank You, Gravity!

생각의 폭을 넓히는 배경지식 Story

#Topic Muscles & Bones

우리가 움직이거나, 음식을 먹고 소화하거나, 숨을 쉴 때 필요한 것이 바로 muscle이에요. muscle이라는 말은 작은 쥐라는 의미를 담고 있는 라틴어 머스큘러스(musculus)에서 유래했다고 해요. 피부 아래 일부 근육이 마치 작은 쥐처럼 움직인다고 해서 붙은 이름이랍니다.

먼저 근육의 구조를 살펴보면, elbow를 straighten하는 것과 같이 우리 bone에 fasten되어 우리의 의지대로 움직이는 근육인 skeletal muscles와 우리의 의지와 상관없이 자율신경으로 조절되는 근육인 내장근과 심근이 있어요. 특히 심근은 우리 몸에서 가장 부지런한 근육이라고 할 수 있어요. 또, 골격근과 심근에는 가로무늬가 있지만, 가로무늬가 없는 것을 민무늬근이라고 해요. 이 smooth muscles에는 내장근이 대표적이랍니다.

만약 우리가 space 정거장과 같이 gravity가 없는 곳에 오래 머무르게 되면 근육이 퇴화한다고 해요. 그래서 astronaut들은 무중력 상태에서도 treadmill 등의 machine을 이용해 꾸준히 운동을 해요. 또, 우리는 얼굴을 찡그릴 때보다 웃을 때 더 많은 근육을 사용한다는 사실을 아시나요? 그래서 자주 웃으면 얼굴 근육을 많이 사용하기 때문에 근육이 단단해지면서 좀 더 젊은 얼굴을 유지할 수 있다고 해요. 지금부터 웃으면서 근육에 대해 배워볼까요?

본문 미리보기 QUIZ

1 우리 몸에는 600개 이상의 [□ 뼈 / □ 근육] 이/가 있다. 82쪽에서 확인

2 무중력 상태에서 우주 비행사들은 [□ 운동할 필요가 없다. / □ 열심히 운동해야 한다.] 84쪽에서 확인

독해의 장벽을 깨는 만만한 Vocabulary

Study Date: ____ / ____

☐ 1	**astronaut** [ǽstrənɔ̀:t]	명 우주 비행사	우주 비행사가 되다	become an ________
☐ 2	**bend** [bend]	동 구부리다, 굽히다	무릎을 구부리다	________ your knees
☐ 3	**bone** [boun]	명 뼈	부러진 뼈	a broken ________
☐ 4	**buckle** [bʌ́kl]	명 버클, 죔쇠	금속 버클	a metal ________
☐ 5	**combination** [kɑ̀mbənéiʃən]	명 결합	색깔들의 조합	a ________ of colors
☐ 6	**elbow** [élbou]	명 팔꿈치	오른쪽 팔꿈치	your right ________
☐ 7	**fasten** [fǽsn]	동 묶다, 붙들어 매다	안전벨트를 매다	________ your seat belt
☐ 8	**machine** [məʃí:n]	명 기계 장치	복사기	a copy ________
☐ 9	**muscle** [mʌ́sl]	명 근육	근육 통증	________ pain
☐ 10	**skeletal** [skélətl]	형 골격의	골격 근육	________ muscles
☐ 11	**smooth** [smu:ð]	형 매끄러운	민무늬 근육	________ muscles
☐ 12	**straighten** [stréitn]	동 똑바르게 펴다	다리를 똑바르게 펴라	________ your legs
☐ 13	**strap** [stræp]	동 끈으로 매다	단단하게 묶다	________ tightly
☐ 14	**treadmill** [trédmìl]	명 러닝머신	러닝머신에서 뛰다	run on a ________
☐ 15	**wheel** [*h*wi:l]	명 바퀴	앞바퀴	a front ________

어휘 자신만만 QUIZ

1 골격근은 뼈에 붙어 있다.

Skeletal muscles are ____________ to bones.

2 그들은 기계 장치에 그들 자신을 끈으로 묶어야 한다.

They have to ____________ themselves to the machine.

Reading 01 Muscles at Work

My Reading Time | Words 158 / 1분 45초

1회 ____분____초 2회 ____분____초

Each person has more than six hundred muscles. They are all over your body. Interestingly, about one hundred of them are in your face and neck alone. They let you laugh, close your eyes, and eat food.

Some of the muscles, called skeletal muscles, are fastened to bones. They usually work in pairs because a muscle can only pull, but not push. Skeletal muscles take turns pulling bones when you bend and straighten your elbow or when you open and close your mouth.

There are also smooth muscles. They work without your thinking about them. For example, smooth muscles in your eyes change the size of your pupils. Other smooth muscles help your body make use of the food you eat. Others help the blood move through your body.

Muscles work for you in special ways, sometimes alone and sometimes in combination. Even though you may not notice it or think about it, they are always at work.

Words muscle 명 근육 neck 명 목 skeletal 형 골격의 fasten 동 묶다, 붙들어 매다 bone 명 뼈 pair 명 쌍[짝] bend 동 구부리다 straighten 동 똑바르게 하다, 펴다 elbow 명 팔꿈치 smooth 형 매끄러운 pupil 명 동공 blood 명 피, 혈액 combination 명 결합 notice 동 알아채다

Study Date: ____ / ____

LINK 실력 향상 WORKBOOK p.38

Topic

1 본문의 주제로 가장 알맞은 것은?

a. bones and muscles

b. human muscles in the face

c. types and functions of muscles

d. the number of muscles in the body

Inference

2 다음과 같이 추론할 때, 빈칸에 들어갈 말로 가장 알맞은 것은?

> Skeletal muscles don't work when ________________.

a. your pupils get bigger

b. you walk up and down the stairs

c. your mouth is opened and closed

d. you bend and straighten your elbow

Reference

3 밑줄 친 they가 가리키는 것은?

a. bones b. muscles c. ways d. pupils

Summary

4 **Complete the summary with the words in the box.**

think	body	muscles	smooth	skeletal	pull

We have over 600 muscles in our ________. There are two types: ________ and smooth muscles. Skeletal muscles are fastened to bones. They can only ________, not push. But ________ muscles work even when we don't ________ about them.

지식 백과

근육의 중요성

인간의 경우, 600개가 넘는 근육은 전체 몸무게의 45% 정도를 차지한다. 뼈의 무게 비중이 약 12%라는 점을 고려할 때 우리 몸에는 엄청난 근육이 숨어 있는 것이다. 근육은 우리가 움직일 수 있도록 해줄 뿐만 아니라 에너지를 태우는 역할을 한다. 체내에 근육의 양이 많은 사람들은 대체로 기초대사량(활동을 하지 않을 때 소모되는 열량)이 높기 때문에, 똑같은 양의 음식을 먹어도 살이 덜 찐다. 근육은 사용하면 할수록 강해지는 특징을 가진다.

근육은 어떻게 커지는지 동영상으로 알아보세요. Time 4' 14"

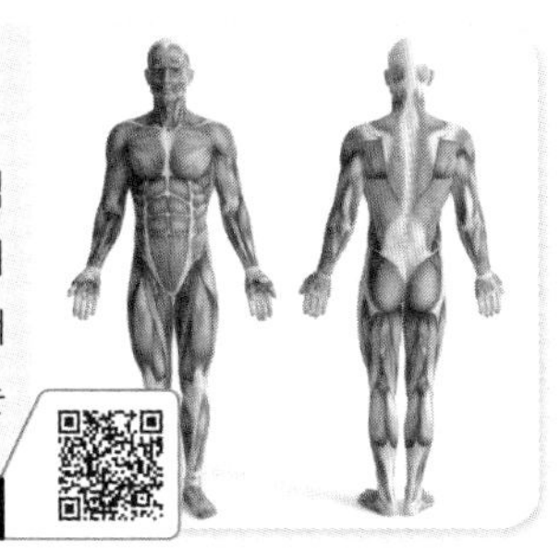

Reading 02 Exercise in Space

My Reading Time | Words 171 / 2분 00초

1회 ____분____초 2회 ____분____초

On Earth, even during sleep, the human body moves against the force of gravity. We use muscles and bones to fight gravity. Thus, our body always gets lots of exercise. In space, however, the human body doesn't have to fight gravity because outer space is free from gravity. So, muscles and bones can easily ________. That is why astronauts have to exercise every day to stay healthy. Exercise is one of the most important things they do during their time in space.

To exercise, astronauts use machines such as treadmills and special bikes. They run on the treadmill. Because there is no gravity in space, they can float in the air. So, they have to strap themselves to the machine.

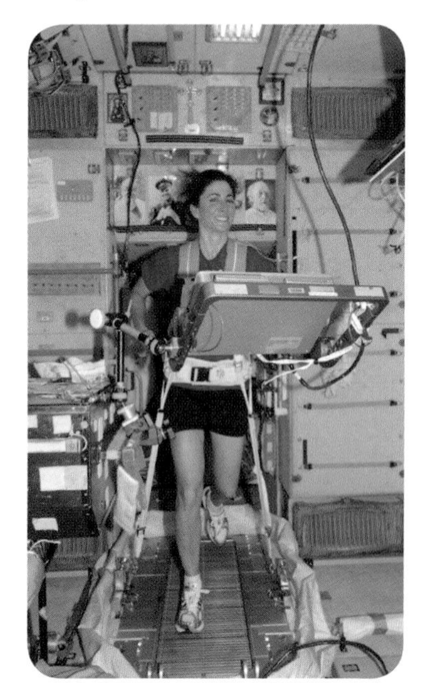

The exercise bike, called the *cycle ergometer, is a machine similar to a bicycle without wheels. They strap their shoes into buckles and wear seat belts to hold themselves down. If astronauts don't exercise enough in space, they may have a hard time getting used to life back on Earth.

*cycle ergometer 고정식 자전거

Words

space 명 우주 force 명 힘 gravity 명 중력 outer 형 외부의 free from ~의 염려가 없는
weak 형 약한 astronaut 명 우주 비행사 machine 명 기계 장치 treadmill 명 러닝머신
float 동 뜨다 strap 동 끈으로 매다 similar 형 비슷한 wheel 명 바퀴 buckle 명 버클, 죔쇠

LINK 실력 향상 WORKBOOK p.40

Main Idea

1 What is the main idea of the passage?

a. There is no gravity in outer space.

b. Muscles and bones get used to gravity.

c. Astronauts exercise in space to stay healthy.

d. The cycle ergometer is a useful machine in space.

Inference

2 빈칸에 들어갈 말로 가장 알맞은 것은?

a. break up

b. get tired

c. fight gravity

d. become weak

Details

3 문장을 읽고 본문의 내용과 일치하면 T, 일치하지 않으면 F를 쓰시오.

(1) ______ Humans use muscles and bones to fight gravity on Earth.

(2) ______ Astronauts feel more gravity in space than on Earth.

(3) ______ When using a treadmill, astronauts have to strap themselves down.

Graphic Organizer

4 본문의 단어를 이용하여 지구와 우주에 관한 표를 완성하시오.

On Earth		In space
There is gravity. ⇩ We use muscles and bones to fight ________. ⇩ Our body gets lots of ________.	V.S.	There is no ________. ⇩ Astronauts' muscles and bones become ________. ⇩ They have to ________ every day using a ________ or a cycle ergometer.

지식 백과

무중력이란?

무중력이란 만유인력(질량을 가지고 있는 모든 물체가 서로 잡아당기는 힘) 및 원심력(물체가 회전하면서 멀어져 가려는 힘) 등의 관성력(물체가 운동 상태를 유지하려는 힘)이 서로 작용하여 그 합이 0 내지는 0으로 간주되는 정도로 작아진 상태를 일컫는다. 무중력이란 중력이 완전히 사라지는 게 아니라 중력을 느낄 수 없는 상태나 물체에 중력이 작용하지 않는 것처럼 보이는 현상이다. 무중력 환경은 우주에서 자연적으로 발견될 뿐만 아니라, 자유낙하 등을 통해 인공적으로 조성할 수도 있다. 무중력 상태에서는 대류 현상이 없으므로 바람도 불지 않는다.

Reading Closer

독해의 내공을 키우는 마무리 학습

A Unit 10에서 학습한 단어를 생각해 보고, 다음 퍼즐을 완성해 보시오.

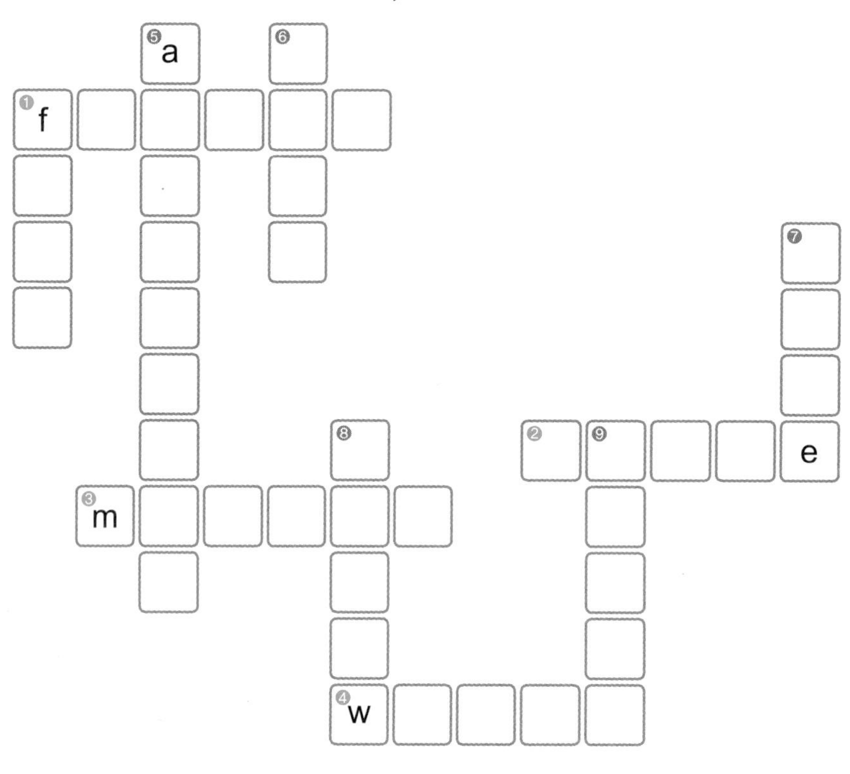

Across

❶ 안전벨트를 매다: __________ your seat belt

❷ 우주 정거장: a __________ station

❸ a piece of tissue to connect two bones when you move

❹ 바퀴를 수리하다: repair the __________

Down

❶ Outer space is __________ from gravity.
(우주 공간은 중력이 없다.)

❺ a person who travels in a spacecraft into outer space

❻ not strong

❼ the hard parts inside your body which together form your skeleton

❽ 팔꿈치를 펴라: straighten your __________

❾ 눈동자; 학생

B 다음 [보기]에서 알맞은 말을 골라 문장을 완성하시오.

보기	similar	force	combination	pair	blood

1 Rama and Sita used to be a very happy __________.

2 I use a __________ of various methods for teaching math.

3 The elderly woman lost a lot of __________ in the accident.

4 Many houses were destroyed by the strong __________ of the wind.

5 The brothers look so __________ that I cannot tell one from the other.

생각을 키우는 서술형 • 수행평가 대비 훈련

C 다음 네모 안에서 알맞은 말을 골라 글을 완성하시오.

Each person has hundreds of [muscles / bones]. Without them, we cannot [fasten / bend] our elbow or open our mouth. Even during sleep, we use them to fight [gravity / disease]. In space, however, there is no such force, and muscles do not get enough [exercise / energy]. Therefore, [astronauts / scientists] use machines to exercise in space. This helps them stay healthy.

UNIT 11 Home Alone

생각의 폭을 넓히는 **배경지식 Story**

#*Topic* Single-Person Household

"밥 먹었니? 밥 먹고 다녀라. 밥 한번 먹자…." 우리는 '밥'을 먹는 것을 중요하게 생각하죠. 그런데 이 밥 문화가 최근 조금씩 바뀌고 있어요. 여러 사람과 함께 식사하는 것에서 벗어나 혼자 식사하는 것을 선호하는 사람이 늘고 있는데, 이것을 '혼밥'이라고 불러요. 최근에는 혼밥이 많은 사람들 사이에서 점차 trend로 자리 잡았죠.

혼밥 문화가 널리 퍼지게 된 데에는 여러 가지 이유가 있겠지만, single-person household가 증가한 것이 주된 원인이에요. 2017년 통계청 research 자료에 따르면 우리나라의 1인 가구 rate은 약 28%로, 2000년에 15.5%였던 것보다 훨씬 증가한 수치라고 해요. 1인 가구가 총 population에서 차지하는 percentage는 지난 17년간 계속 증가하는 추세예요. expert들은 이런 현상이 앞으로도 계속 될 것이라고 predict하고 있고요. 다시 말하면 혼자 밥을 먹고, 혼자 물건을 사고, 혼자 문화생활을 즐기는 사람들이 더 늘어날 거라는 이야기예요.

그래서 요즘은 이런 '혼족', 즉 혼자 생활하는 사람들을 겨냥한 상품이 많이 나오고 있어요. 가까운 convenience store에서 파는 convenience 음식이 대표적이죠. 또한 이런 간편식들을 조합해서 맛있는 '편의점 요리'를 만드는 것이 사람들 사이에 유행하기도 하고요. 이런 모두가 우리 사회의 변화를 반영하는 움직임이라고 할 수 있어요.

본문 미리보기 QUIZ

1 프랑스 파리에서는 인구의 [☐ 절반 / ☐ 대부분]이 혼자 살고 있다. 90쪽에서 확인

2 쉽게 요리가 가능한 음식을 [☐ convenience food / ☐ special package]라고 한다. 92쪽에서 확인

Study Date: ______ / ______

☐ 1	**contain** [kəntéin]	통 포함하다	많은 염분을 포함하다	________ much salt
☐ 2	**convenience** [kənvíːnjəns]	명 편리, 편의	편의점	a ________ store
☐ 3	**divorce** [divɔ́ːrs]	명 이혼	이혼하다	get a ________
☐ 4	**expert** [ékspəːrt]	명 전문가	의학 전문가	a medical ________
☐ 5	**freeze** [friːz]	통 얼리다, 냉동하다	수프를 얼리다	________ the soup
☐ 6	**nutrient** [njúːtriənt]	명 영양소	필수 영양소	an essential ________
☐ 7	**overall** [óuvərɔ́ːl]	부 전체적으로	전체적으로 긍정적이다	be positive ________
☐ 8	**package** [pǽkidʒ]	명 포장	작은 포장	a small ________
☐ 9	**percentage** [pərséntidʒ]	명 백분율, 비율	손님의 비율	the ________ of customers
☐ 10	**population** [pɑ̀pjuléiʃən]	명 인구	인구 문제	a ________ problem
☐ 11	**predict** [pridíkt]	통 예상하다	날씨를 예측하다	________ the weather
☐ 12	**rate** [reit]	명 비율	평균 비율	the average ________
☐ 13	**research** [ríːsəːrtʃ]	명 조사	조사 업체	a ________ company
☐ 14	**technology** [teknɑ́lədʒi]	명 기술	현대의 기술	modern ________
☐ 15	**trend** [trend]	명 추세, 경향	사회적 추세[트렌드]	a social ________

어휘 자신만만 QUIZ

1 전문가들은 그 추세가 계속될 것이라고 예상한다.

Experts ____________ the trend will continue.

2 새로운 기술 덕분에, 우리는 영양소를 잃지 않고 음식을 얼릴 수 있다.

Thanks to new ____________, we can freeze foods without losing ____________.

Reading 01

Living Alone

My Reading Time | Words 174 / 2분 00초

1회 ____분 ____초 2회 ____분 ____초

The single-person household is a growing trend. More and more people are living alone. According to Euromonitor, a research company in the United Kingdom, the number of single-person households in the world went up by 33 percent in just ten years. The report also says that almost one in every ten households has just one person. The rate is much higher in big cities. In France, nearly half of the population in Paris lives alone.

Overall, the percentage of single-person households is far greater in developed nations. For example, one in three households in the United States has just one person. The rate is far (A) [lower / higher] in developing nations. In South America, for instance, only about 7% of all households are single-person. In Africa, the rate is much lower — close to 3%.

Experts predict the trend will continue. People live longer, and the number of older people who live alone is increasing. Also, people tend to marry (B) [earlier / later], and divorce is becoming more common. For various reasons, more people are choosing to live alone.

Words

household 명 세대, 가족 trend 명 유행, 경향 according to …에 따르면 research 명 조사
population 명 인구 overall 부 전체적으로 percentage 명 백분율, 비율 developed 형 발전된
rate 명 비율 for instance 예를 들어 expert 명 전문가 predict 동 예상하다 divorce 명 이혼

LINK 실력 향상 WORKBOOK p.42

Title

1 **본문의 다른 제목으로 가장 알맞은 것은?**

a. Those Who Live Alone

b. Single-person Households on the Rise

c. Problems of Single-person Households

d. Single-person Households in Big Cities

Words

2 **(A)와 (B)에 들어갈 알맞은 단어를 본문에서 찾아 쓰시오.**

(A) → ____________________

(B) → ____________________

Inference

3 **밑줄 친 trend에 해당하지 않는 것은?**

a. Dohun: More people are getting married at older ages.

b. Yuna: More and more families want to have just one kid.

c. Sangsik: Old people live longer than before.

d. Nari: The divorce rate is going up.

Graphic Organizer

4 **본문의 단어를 이용하여 표를 완성하시오.**

The Increase in Single-person Households

• Almost one in __________ households • Greater in big cities and __________ nations – almost __________ % in Paris – about 33% in the United States	Reasons • People live __________. • People marry __________. • More people divorce.

지식 백과

1인 가구

통계청의 2018년 발표에 따르면, 우리나라에서는 1인 가구가 2015년에 이미 전체 가구 중 27.2%로 주된 가구 형태가 되었고, 2017년에는 전체 가구(1,967만)의 28.6%를 차지하였다. 성별로 보면, 1인 가구 중에서 279만 가구는 남자이며, 283만 가구는 여자로 나타났다. 아울러, '사별'로 인한 1인 가구의 비율은 감소하였으나, '이혼'으로 인한 1인 가구의 비중은 증가하는 추세이다.

1인 가구에 대한 전망을 동영상으로 알아보세요. Time 2' 07"

Reading 02 Convenience Foods

My Reading Time | Words 155 / 1분 45초

1회 ____분 ____초 2회 ____분 ____초

As more and more people are living alone, there is growing need for foods that can be easily cooked. These foods are called "convenience foods." They come in small packages. They are always easy to buy and ready to use. Put them in your microwave oven for a few minutes, and you will have a tasty meal. Convenience foods are becoming popular among people who live alone or have little time to cook.

Thanks to new technology, people can freeze vegetables, fruit, meat, and fish without losing many nutrients. They can also keep foods fresh in special packages.

________, convenience foods have some problems because the foods are less healthy. Many of them contain more salt than the food you make at home. Also, they often include more chemicals that may not be good for your health. So, read food labels carefully. Also, you should not eat convenience foods more than twice a week.

Words

convenience 명 편리, 편의 package 명 포장 microwave oven 전자레인지 tasty 형 맛있는
thanks to …덕분에 technology 명 기술 freeze 동 얼리다, 냉동하다 nutrient 명 영양소
contain 동 담고 있다, 내포하다 include 동 포함하다 chemical 명 화학 물질

LINK 실력 향상 WORKBOOK p.44

1 Inference

필자의 충고로 가장 알맞은 것은?

a. Keep away from chemicals.

b. Be careful with convenience foods.

c. Learn how to cook convenience foods.

d. Keep your food fresh for better nutrition.

2 Linking

빈칸에 들어갈 말로 가장 알맞은 것은?

a. Finally b. Therefore c. Also d. However

3 Details

convenience foods에 관한 설명을 읽고 본문의 내용과 일치하면 T, 일치하지 않으면 F를 쓰시오.

(1) ______ They are popular among people who love cooking.

(2) ______ Various foods can be made into them.

(3) ______ They usually contain a lot of salt and chemicals.

4 Summary

Complete the summary with the words in the box.

expensive	nutrient	time	salt	money	popular

Convenience foods are becoming ________ these days. Single-person households or people who have little ________ to cook love to buy them. New technology can be used to produce convenience foods without ________ loss. But they often have more ________ and chemicals that may not be good for your health. So, you should not depend too much on them.

지식 백과

식품 라벨(food label)

식품 라벨에는 제품명, 제조연월일, 유통기한, 품질 유지 기한, 원재료, 식품 첨가물, 영양 성분, 열량, 1회 제공량 등이 기재되어 있다. 이를 통해 생산자는 건강한 식생활을 위한 정확한 정보를 제공하고, 소비자는 자신에게 적합한 식품을 선택할 수 있다. 가령, 라면을 먹더라도 건강을 생각한다면, 기름에 튀기지 않은 비유탕면과 나트륨 함량이 적은 것을 선택하는 것이 좋다. 보통 라면 1개당 나트륨 함량은 평균 2,075mg으로 세계보건기구(WHO)에서 정한 성인 1일 권장량인 1,968mg을 넘는다.

Reading Closer

독해의 내공을 키우는 **마무리 학습**

A

Unit 11에서 학습한 단어를 생각해 보고, 다음 퍼즐을 완성해 보시오.

Across

❶ You are not ________. (너는 혼자가 아니야.)

❷ a careful study that is done to find new knowledge about something

❸ 선진국: a ________ country

❹ Eating too much ________ is bad for your health.
(너무 많은 염분을 먹는 것은 건강에 좋지 않다.)

❺ 경향, 트렌드

Down

❻ 출생률, 출생 비율: the birth ________

❼ a substance that plants, animals, and people need to live and grow

❽ to say that something will or might happen in the future

❾ a person who has special skills or knowledge relating to a particular subject

❿ one of two equal parts of anything; 50%

B

다음 [보기]에서 알맞은 말을 골라 문장을 완성하시오.

보기 contain nutrient divorce population common

1 Vitamin C is an essential __________ for the human body.

2 Since getting a __________, he has been raising his son alone.

3 Ginger is a very __________ ingredient in Chinese cooking.

4 Young children should avoid foods that __________ too much fat.

5 As people continue to have fewer children, the country's __________ will go down.

생각을 키우는 서술형 • 수행평가 대비 훈련

C

다음 [보기]에서 알맞은 말을 골라 글을 완성하시오.

The single-person household is a growing __________. According to recent research, the number of single-person households in the world __________ by 33 percent in just ten years. Experts __________ the trend will continue and affect society in various ways. For example, as more people __________ to live alone, there is a growing need for __________ foods. Eating such foods too much can cause problems because they are less healthy.

보기 convenience trend increased choose predict

UNIT 12 The Joy of Reading

생각의 폭을 넓히는 **배경지식 Story**

#*Topic* Reading Novels

여러분은 「80일 간의 세계 일주」라는 책을 읽어 본 적이 있나요? 이 책은 1873년에 출간된 novel이고, author는 쥘 베른이에요. 요즘이야 며칠이면 세계 일주를 할 수 있지만 당시만 해도 비행기가 없었기 때문에 상상하기 힘든 일이었다고 해요. 쥘 베른은 adventure 소설을 즐겨 썼던 영국의 유명한 작가였어요.

사실 novel이라는 문학 장르는 태어난 지 오래되지 않았어요. 희곡이나 시는 고대로부터 있던 오래된 문학 장르이지만 소설이 본격적으로 쓰이기 시작한 것은 17세기경이라고 해요. 17~18세기 유럽에서는 산업 혁명이 일어나고 이로 인해 중산 계급이 새롭게 만들어져요. 이들은 귀족들이 즐기던 희곡이나 시보다는 쉽게 읽고 이해할 수 있는 이야기에 관심이 많았어요. 이때 많은 소설이 신문에 연재되기도 했는데, author가 독자들의 opinion 때문에 소설의 character를 죽이지 않게 하는 등 결말을 바꾸는 일도 많았다고 해요. 우리 TV 드라마도 간혹 시청자들의 항의에 결말이 바뀌는 것처럼요.

우리도 조선 시대 후기에 이르러서 소설이 대중적으로 널리 읽혔다고 해요. 특히 소설을 읽어주는 사람, 이른바 전기수(傳奇叟)라는 직업도 출현했는데요, 이들은 이야기의 절정 부분에 이르러서는 갑자기 책 읽기를 탁! 멈추었다고 해요. 그러면 뒷이야기가 궁금해진 사람들이 앞다투어 돈을 던졌어요. 어찌나 실감나게 읽었던지 전기수를 소설 속 나쁜 character로 오인하고 해를 입히는 사람도 있었다고 하네요. 자, 그러면 이제 책 읽기에 관한 글을 읽어 볼까요?

본문 미리보기 QUIZ

1 책을 다 읽고 나서 쓰는 것은 [□ book report / □ paragraph]이다. 98쪽에서 확인

2 「80일 간의 세계 일주」의 주인공 필리어스 포그는 [□ 런던 / □ 파리]에 살았다. 100쪽에서 확인

Study Date: ______ / ______

	Word	Meaning	예시	Phrase
☐ 1	**adventure** [ədvéntʃər]	명 모험	모험 소설	an ________ novel
☐ 2	**argue** [á:rgju:]	동 논쟁하다	그녀와 논쟁하다	________ with her
☐ 3	**author** [ɔ́:θər]	명 작가	그 책의 작가	________ of the book
☐ 4	**bet** [bet]	동 내기를 하다	100달러 내기하다	________ $100
☐ 5	**character** [kǽriktər]	명 등장인물	주요 등장인물	the major ________
☐ 6	**expect** [ikspékt]	동 예상하다, 기대하다	성공하기를 기대하다	________ to succeed
☐ 7	**novel** [návəl]	명 소설	소설을 읽다	read a ________
☐ 8	**opinion** [əpínjən]	명 의견	긍정적인 의견	a positive ________
☐ 9	**prepare** [pripέər]	동 준비하다	미래를 대비하다	________ for the future
☐ 10	**recommend** [rèkəménd]	동 추천하다	이 책을 추천하다	________ this book
☐ 11	**sleigh** [slei]	명 썰매	썰매를 타다	ride a ________
☐ 12	**solution** [səlú:ʃən]	명 해결책	해결책을 찾다	find a ________
☐ 13	**take notes**	받아 적다, 메모하다	결과를 메모하다	________ of the result
☐ 14	**whether** [hwéðər]	접 ~인지 아닌지	그게 사실인지 아닌지	________ it is true
☐ 15	**yacht** [jɑt]	명 요트	요트 경주	a ________ race

어휘 자신만만 QUIZ

1 당신은 다른 사람들에게 그 책을 추천하겠는가?

Would you ____________ the book to others?

2 그는 요트, 썰매, 심지어 코끼리까지 타야만 했다.

He had to ride ____________, sleighs, and even elephants.

Reading 01

Writing a Book Report

My Reading Time | Words 175 / 2분 00초

1회 ____분____초 2회 ____분____초

Writing a book report is a common problem for many students. A book report gives information about a book such as the title, the author, and a summary of the book. It also gives an opinion about the book. To write a good book report, there are some important steps that you need to follow.

5 First of all, choose a book you like. If you are interested in the book, you can understand it much more easily. Second, take notes as you read. Prepare a pen and paper before you start reading and take notes about the characters and main ideas. Third, write a paragraph summarizing the story. You need to write about the main characters, their problems, and their 10 solutions. Lastly, write a paragraph about your opinion of the book. You can write about your favorite part or what you learned.

Remember that every good report answers this important question: Would you recommend the book to others? After reading 15 your report, people should be able to decide if they want to read the book.

Words

common 형 흔한, 공통의 information 명 정보 author 명 작가 opinion 명 의견 take notes 메모하다 prepare 동 준비하다 character 명 등장인물 paragraph 명 단락 summarize 동 요약하다 solution 명 해결책 remember 동 기억하다 recommend 동 추천하다 decide 동 결정하다

Study Date: ______ / ______

LINK 실력 향상 WORKBOOK p.46

1 Purpose

What is the purpose of the passage?

a. to explain how to write a book report

b. to encourage people to read more books

c. to show an example of a good book report

d. to emphasize the importance of taking notes

2 Details

독후감에 포함시킬 필요가 없는 것은?

a. writer's name

b. main ideas

c. reader's opinion

d. reasonable price

3 Words

주어진 정의에 해당하는 단어를 본문에서 찾아 쓰시오.

people in books, plays, films, and so on → ______________

4 Graphic Organizer

본문의 단어를 이용하여 표를 완성하시오.

Writing a Book Report

Step 1	Step 2	Step 3	Step 4
Choose a book you are ________ in.	Take notes about ________ and main ideas.	________ the story. Write about characters, problems, and solutions.	Write your ________ of the book.

지식백과

조사 보고서의 색

백서(white book)는 정부가 특정 사안이나 주제에 대해서 조사한 결과를 정리하여 발표하는 종합 보고서이다. 영국 정부가 만들어 의회에 제출한 보고서의 표지를 하얀색으로 한 데에서 그 명칭이 유래하였다. 나라마다 보고서의 표지가 다르기 때문에 yellow book(프랑스), green book(이탈리아), orange book(네덜란드), grey book(일본) 등의 이름이 쓰인다.

Reading 02

Around the World in 80 Days

My Reading Time | Words 176 / 2분 00초

1회 ____분____초 2회 ____분____초

Around the World in 80 Days is an adventure novel by Jules Verne. It is about a man who went around the world in only 80 days. His name was Phileas Fogg. He was a rich man who lived in London. One day, he argued with his friends about whether a man could go around the world in 80 days. He bet £20,000 that he could do it.

Traveling around the world in 80 days is not a problem today. But there were no airplanes at that time. Mr. Fogg had to ride trains, steam boats, yachts, sleighs, and even elephants. However, Mr. Fogg arrived home a few minutes later than he expected. He thought he had lost all his money. But there was one more day left.

The idea that Mr. Fogg gained one day was my favorite part of the book. He gained one day because he traveled east and crossed the International Date Line. This is the part that makes the book not just an adventure story. It is based on science, too.

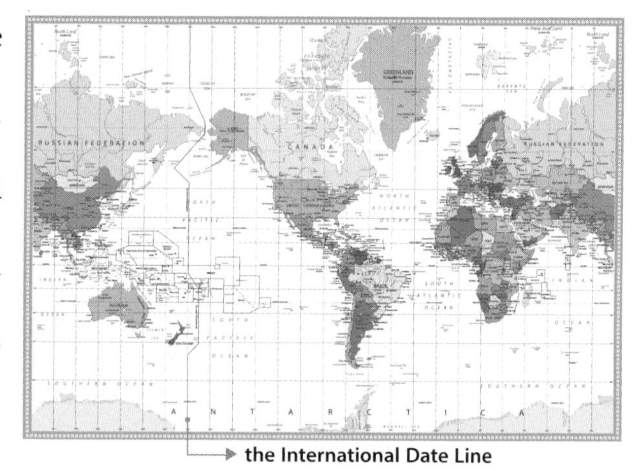

the International Date Line

Words adventure 명 모험 novel 명 소설 rich 형 부유한 argue 동 논쟁하다 whether 접 …인지 아닌지 bet 동 내기를 하다 steam boat 증기선 yacht 명 요트 sleigh 명 썰매 expect 동 예상하다 gain 동 얻다 cross 동 건너다 be based on …을 기반으로 하다

Study Date: ______ / ______

LINK 실력 향상 WORKBOOK p.48

1 Text Type

글의 종류로 가장 알맞은 것은?

a. diary　　b. book report　　c. biography　　d. news article

2 Details

Fogg 씨가 이용한 교통수단이 아닌 것은?

a. airplanes　　b. trains　　c. sleighs　　d. elephants

3 Details

다음을 읽고 본문의 내용과 일치하면 T, 일치하지 않으면 F를 쓰시오.

(1) ______ *Around the World in 80 Days* was written by Jules Verne.

(2) ______ Mr. Fogg's friends agreed that a man could go around the world in 80 days.

(3) ______ Mr. Fogg lost all his money during the trip.

4 Summary

Complete the summary with the words in the box.

author	novel	one day	science	international	80

• Title : *Around the World in 80 Days*

• ________ : Jules Verne　　• Genre : adventure ________

• Summary : Phileas Fogg bet £20,000 that he could travel around the world in ________ days. However, he arrived home a few minutes later than he expected. At the last moment, he realized that he gained ________ because he crossed the ________ Date Line. He won the bet.

지식백과

Jules Verne(1828~1905)

쥘 베른은 프랑스 낭트에서 태어난 소설가이다. 그는 공상 과학 소설 분야를 개척한 작가로 유명하며, 「지구 속 여행」, 「해저 2만리」, 「80일 간의 세계 일주」와 같은 소설을 남겼다. 쥘 베른은 비행기, 우주선, 잠수함이 만들어지기도 전에 우주, 하늘, 해저 여행에 대한 이야기로 독자의 관심을 끌었다. 그의 작품은 영화로 만들어졌으며, 지금도 많은 독자들이 그의 작품을 사랑하고 있다.

「80일 간의 세계 일주」 영화 예고편 동영상을 감상하세요. Time 1' 34''

Reading Closer

독해의 내공을 키우는 **마무리 학습**

A Unit 12에서 학습한 단어를 생각해 보고, 다음 퍼즐을 완성해 보시오.

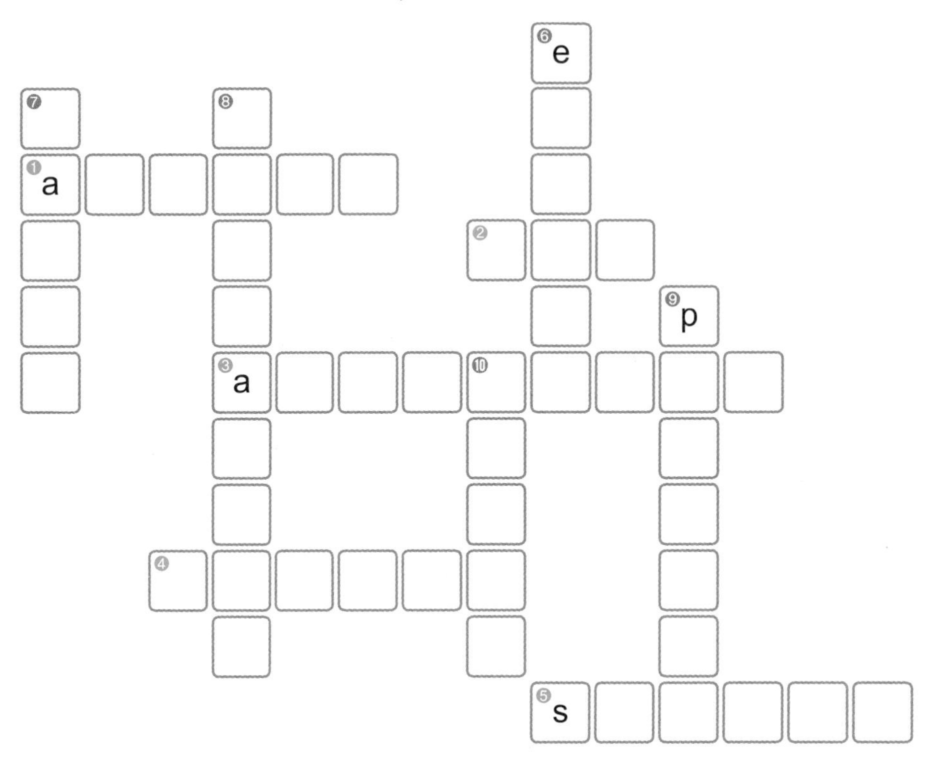

Across

❶ a person who has written something

❷ 내기, 도박; 내기를 하다

❸ an exciting or dangerous experience

❹ 결심하다, 결정하다(to make a choice about something)

❺ an open vehicle that is usually pulled by a horse over snow or ice

Down

❻ 당신을 곧 보기를 기대한다: ________ to see you soon

❼ a large boat that is used for racing or pleasure

❽ 영화의 주인공: the main ________ in the film

❾ to get ready for some activity, purpose, use, etc.

❿ 대중 소설: a popular ________

B 다음 [보기]에서 알맞은 말을 골라 문장을 완성하시오.

보기	argue	cross	opinion	solution	remember

1 Who is the best baseball player in your __________?

2 Scientists are looking for a __________ to the problem.

3 Even close friends often __________ about small things.

4 My grandfather is forgetful, so he cannot __________ things well.

5 The adventurer tried to __________ the narrow part of the river.

생각을 키우는 서술형 • 수행평가 대비 훈련

C 다음 네모 안에서 알맞은 말을 골라 글을 완성하시오.

I wrote a book report about *Around the World in 80 Days*. I chose the [novel / poem] by Jules Verne because I was interested in [money / adventure]. Mr. Phileas Fogg, the book's main [character / author], wanted to prove that he could go around the world in 80 days. It is hard to [summarize / write] the whole book in a few words, but the novel is full of interesting events and surprises. I would strongly [lend / recommend] the book to my friends.

UNIT 13 Interesting Math

생각의 폭을 넓히는 배경지식 Story

#Topic Multiplication

고대 이집트는 수학이 발달해 있었어요. 나일강의 홍수로 인해 농경지를 다시 정비하기 위해서는 정확한 수 개념이 필요했기 때문이죠. 그래서 기원전 2700년경에 10진법이 생겨났고, 더 큰 단위의 수를 add하고 divide하는 method를 발전시킬 수 있었어요.

multiplication table은 이미 2000년 전 중국 한나라 때부터 있었다고 해요. 구구단은 복잡한 수를 multiply할 때 그 답을 calculate하기 쉽도록 도와주는 역할을 했어요. 구구단을 memorize하면, 매번 숫자를 add할 필요가 없거든요.

지난 2011년 옛 백제의 수도였던 부여에서는 구구단표가 적힌 목간(木簡)이 발견되었어요. 목간이란 종이가 발명되기 전에 기록을 위해 사용하던 얇은 나무판을 말해요. 이 목간은 전문가들의 감정 결과 6~7세기의 백제 시대의 것이라 해요. 광개토대왕릉비와 「삼국사기」 등에 구구단과 같은 계산하는 method를 가르쳤다는 기록은 있지만 실제로 구구단표가 적힌 유물이 나온 것은 처음이라고 해요.

그동안 일본은 일제 시대 때 산수 개념이 부족한 조선에 자신들이 multiplication table과 같은 다양한 셈법을 도입시켜 조선인의 눈을 뜨게 했다고 주장했거든요. 더 체계적이고 실용적인 목간의 발견으로 중국에서 만들어진 구구단이 우리나라를 거쳐 일본으로 건너갔음이 증명된 것이죠.

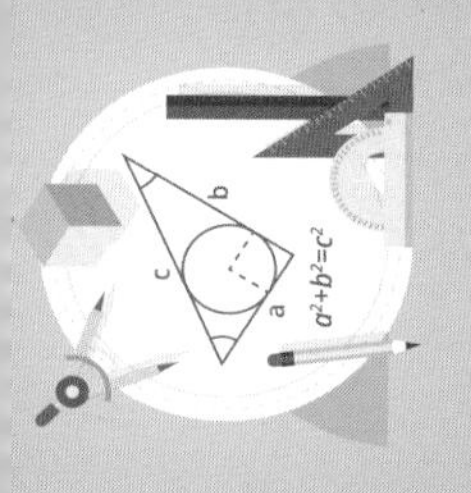

본문 미리보기 QUIZ

1 이집트인들은 큰 수를 곱할 때 먼저, 종이에 [□ 가로 / □ 세로] 선을 그린다. 106쪽에서 확인

2 구구단을 자세히 살펴보면 몇 가지 흥미로운 [□ 패턴을 / □ 오류를] 발견할 수 있다. 108쪽에서 확인

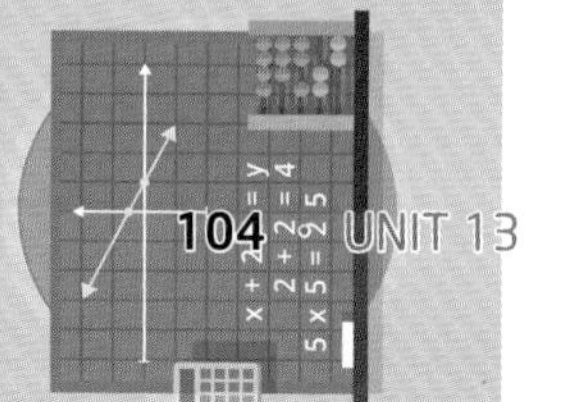

독해의 장벽을 깨는 만만한 Vocabulary

Study Date: ______ / ______

☐ 1	**add** [æd]	동 더하다	수를 모두 더하다	______ up the numbers
☐ 2	**calculate** [kǽlkjulèit]	동 계산하다	평균을 계산하다	______ the average
☐ 3	**calculator** [kǽlkjulèitər]	명 계산기	휴대용 계산기	a pocket ______
☐ 4	**digit** [dídʒit]	명 한 자리 숫자	두 자리 숫자	a two-______ number
☐ 5	**divide** [diváid]	동 나누다	2로 나누다	______ by two
☐ 6	**memorize** [méməràiz]	동 암기하다	그 시를 외우다	______ the poem
☐ 7	**method** [méθəd]	명 방법	과학적인 방법	a scientific ______
☐ 8	**multiplication** [mʌ̀ltəplikéiʃən]	명 곱셈	곱셈표[구구단]	the ______ table
☐ 9	**multiply** [mʌ́ltəplài]	동 곱하다	2와 3을 곱하다	______ two and three
☐ 10	**notice** [nóutis]	동 알아채다	그의 자녀를 알아보다	______ his child
☐ 11	**pattern** [pǽtərn]	명 패턴, 형식	유사한 패턴	a similar ______
☐ 12	**property** [prápərti]	명 특성, 속성	특별한 속성	a special ______
☐ 13	**sum** [sʌm]	명 합계	숫자들의 합계	the ______ of the digits
☐ 14	**suppose** [səpóuz]	동 가정하다	참이라고 가정해 보다	______ that it is true
☐ 15	**underline** [ʌ́ndərlàin]	동 밑줄을 긋다	단어에 밑줄을 긋다	______ the word

어휘 자신만만 QUIZ

1 우리는 계산기 없이 숫자들을 곱할 수 있다.

We can ______ numbers without a calculator.

2 당신은 3×5는 5×3과 같다는 것을 알아차릴 수 있다.

You can ______ that three times five equals five times three.

Reading 01

Egyptian Way to Multiply

My Reading Time | Words 170 / 1분 55초

1회 ____분 ____초 2회 ____분 ____초

When we multiply numbers without a calculator, we use the multiplication table. The multiplication table allows us (A) [calculate / to calculate] numbers easily. But ancient Egyptians used another method, especially for large numbers.

5 Suppose you have this problem: 14 x 28 = ? Draw a line down a piece of paper. On the left side, write 1, 2, 4, 8, 16, and so on. On the right side, write the number you are multiplying by (in this case, 28). Under 28, write 56. That is double 28. Then double 56, and write the number 112 under it. Keep going. Your table should look like this:

1	28
2	56
4	112
8	224
16	448
…	…

10 Now find the numbers on the left side that (B) [add / adds] up to the first number in the problem (in this case, 14). The numbers 2, 4, and 8 add up to 14. Then underline the numbers on the right side opposite these numbers (in this case, 56, 112, 15 and 224). Finally, add these numbers, and you will get 392. This is the answer to 14 x 28.

Words

multiply 동 곱하다 without 전 ~ 없이 calculator 명 계산기 multiplication 명 곱셈 allow 동 허락하다, 가능하게 하다 calculate 동 계산하다 method 명 방법 especially 부 특히 suppose 동 가정하다 double 형 두 배의 add 동 더하다 underline 동 밑줄을 긋다

LINK 실력 향상 WORKBOOK p.50

Topic

1 What is the passage mainly about?

a. the history of calculators

b. a secret hidden in numbers

c. the multiplication method that ancient Egyptians used

d. making the multiplication table that is commonly used today

Grammar

2 (A)와 (B)에 들어갈 말로 어법상 알맞은 것을 골라 쓰시오.

(A): ____________________ (B): ____________________

Inference

3 본문에 소개된 곱하기 방법에 따라 각 빈칸에 알맞은 숫자를 쓰시오.

1	139
2	278
4	556
8	1112
______	2224

28 × __________

= 556 + __________ + 2224

= __________

Graphic Organizer

4 본문의 단어를 이용하여 고대 이집트인들의 곱셈 방법에 관한 표를 완성하시오.

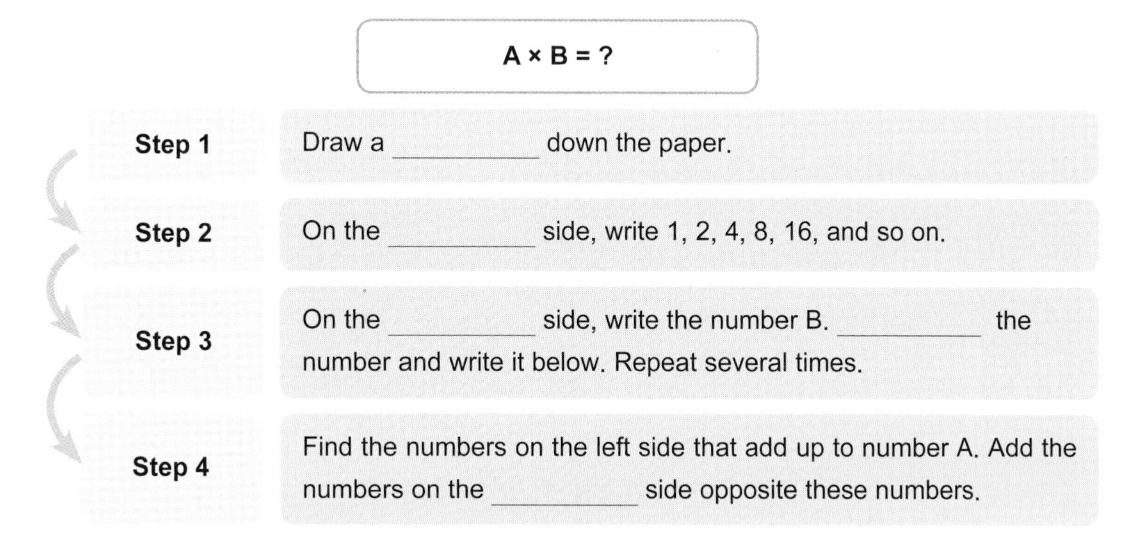

A × B = ?
Step 1
Draw a __________ down the paper.
Step 2
On the __________ side, write 1, 2, 4, 8, 16, and so on.
Step 3
On the __________ side, write the number B. __________ the number and write it below. Repeat several times.
Step 4
Find the numbers on the left side that add up to number A. Add the numbers on the __________ side opposite these numbers.

지식 백과

손가락 숫자

세상 어디에서나 손가락으로 숫자를 표시하는 경우가 많다. 특히, 시장처럼 시끄러운 곳에서는 말보다는 손으로 숫자를 표시하면 혼동할 우려가 적기 때문이다. 하지만 나라마다 손가락을 이용한 숫자 표시가 조금씩 다르므로 유의해야 한다. 가령, 중국에서 1부터 5까지는 우리의 숫자 세기와 크게 다르지 않지만, 6부터 10까지의 손가락 숫자는 대부분 각 숫자의 한자 모양을 흉내 낸 모습이다.

Reading 02

Learning Multiplication

My Reading Time | Words 183 / 2분 00초

1회 ____분 ____초 2회 ____분 ____초

In Korea, students usually memorize the multiplication table. If you look at it carefully, you can find some interesting patterns.

From the multiplication table, you can notice that 3×5 equals 5×3. Wonder why? 3×5 means you have five groups of three.

Put the five groups together. How many do you have? Yes, $3 \times 5 = 15$. Then, divide them into groups of five.

How many groups do you have? Yes, you have ______________. You can find that $A \times B$ is always the same as $B \times A$. This means that you only have to memorize half of the numbers in the table.

	2	3	4	5	6	7	8	9	10	11
2	4	6	8	10	12	14	16	**18**	20	22
3	6	9	12	15	18	21	24	**27**	30	33
4	8	12	16	20	24	28	32	**36**	40	44
5	10	15	20	25	30	35	40	**45**	50	55
6	12	18	24	30	36	42	48	**54**	60	66
7	14	21	28	35	42	49	56	**63**	70	77
8	16	24	32	40	48	56	64	**72**	80	88
9	18	27	36	45	54	63	72	**81**	90	99
10	20	30	40	50	60	70	80	90	100	110
11	22	33	44	55	66	77	88	99	110	121

Here is another interesting pattern. The results in the 9 times table (the red numbers in a row) have a special property: for each result of $9 \times$ a one-digit number, the sum of the digits is 9.

Here is one more fun pattern. Multiplication by 11 is very easy. Can you figure out what is going on here? Add the two digits and place the sum in between them.

$54 \times 11 = 594$

$31 \times 11 = 341$

$54 \times 11 = 5\square4$

$5+4$

Words

memorize 동 암기하다 pattern 명 패턴, 형식 notice 동 알아채다 equal 동 …와 같다 half 명 반 divide 동 나누다 in a row 한 줄로 property 명 특성, 속성 digit 명 한 자리 숫자, 아라비아 숫자 sum 명 합계 figure out 이해하다

Study Date: ______ / ______

LINK 실력 향상 WORKBOOK p.52

1

Title

본문의 다른 제목으로 가장 알맞은 것은?

a. Difficulty of Multiplication

b. Various Ways to Multiply Numbers

c. The History of the Multiplication Table

d. Interesting Patterns in Multiplication

2

Inference

빈칸에 들어갈 말로 가장 알맞은 것은?

a. five groups of three

b. three groups of five

c. fifteen groups of three

d. one group of fifteen

3

Details

다음을 읽고 본문의 내용과 일치하면 T, 일치하지 않으면 F를 쓰시오.

(1) ______ The multiplication table was developed in Korea.

(2) ______ The results in the 9 times table are 9.

(3) ______ When you multiply two numbers, the order does not matter.

4

Summary

Complete the summary with the words in the box.

differs	digits	sum	patterns	equals	multiplication

You can find some interesting __________ in the multiplication table. First, you will see A × B __________ B × A. Second, the sum of the __________ in the results of 9 × a one-digit number is 9. The final pattern is in multiplication by 11. The __________ of the other digits is placed between them.

지식 백과

구구단의 유래

구구단은 1의 단부터 9의 단까지의 곱셈표를 일컫는다. 십진법에 기초한 구구단은 기원전 300년경에 중국에서 만들어져서 우리나라 등에 전래되었다. 우리나라에서는 9단 곱셈표를 주로 이용하지만 인도 등의 나라에서는 19단 곱셈표를 널리 가르치기도 한다. 수학 교육에 대한 열기가 높은 인도에서 시작된 19단 곱셈표가 인도의 유능한 IT 인력을 낳았다고 주장하는 이들도 있다.

친구에게 써먹는 신기한 수학 계산을 동영상으로 감상해 보세요. Time 4' 38''

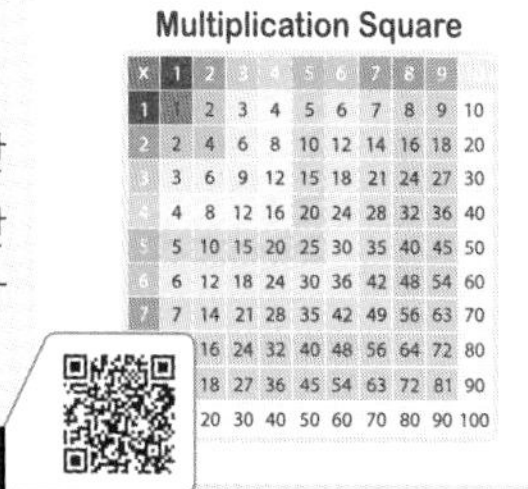

Multiplication Square

×	1	2	3	4	5	6	7	8	9	
1	1	2	3	4	5	6	7	8	9	10
2	2	4	6	8	10	12	14	16	18	20
3	3	6	9	12	15	18	21	24	27	30
4	4	8	12	16	20	24	28	32	36	40
5	5	10	15	20	25	30	35	40	45	50
6	6	12	18	24	30	36	42	48	54	60
7	7	14	21	28	35	42	49	56	63	70
		16	24	32	40	48	56	64	72	80
		18	27	36	45	54	63	72	81	90
		20	30	40	50	60	70	80	90	100

Reading Closer

독해의 내공을 키우는 **마무리 학습**

A Unit 13에서 학습한 단어를 생각해 보고, 다음 퍼즐을 완성해 보시오.

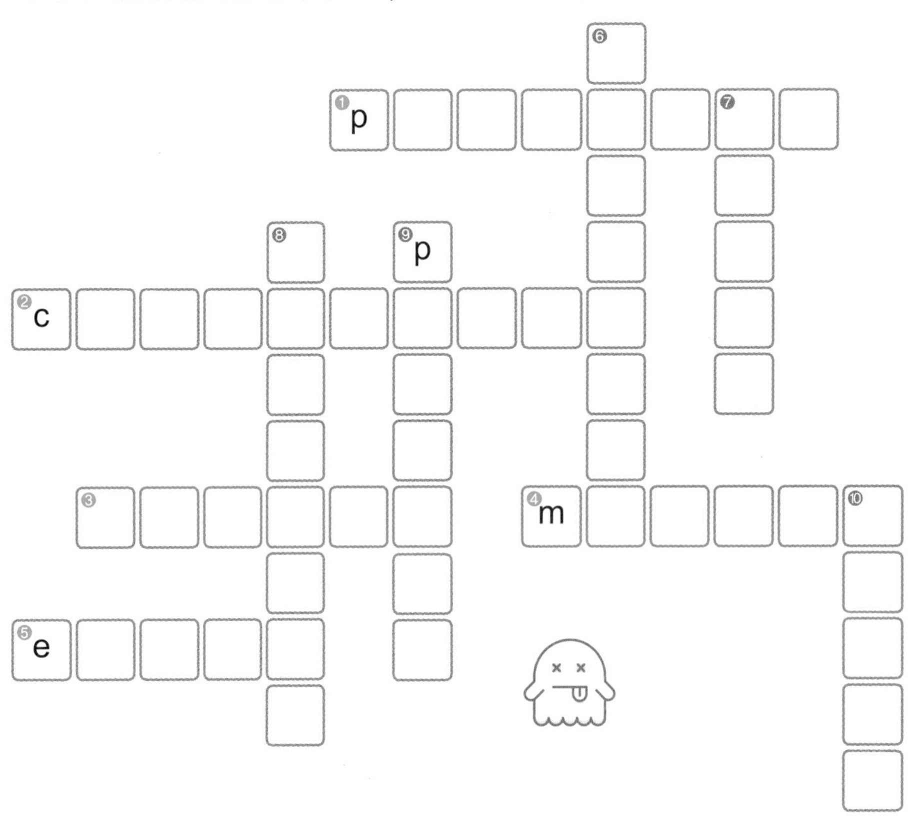

Across

❶ 특성, 속성

❷ a small electronic device that is used for adding, subtracting, etc.

❸ to become aware of something or someone by seeing or hearing

❹ 과학적인 방법: a scientific __________

❺ used to say that one amount or number is the same as another

Down

❻ 영어 단어를 암기하다: __________ English words

❼ 구구단, 곱셈표: the multiplication __________

❽ 곱셈하다

❾ a repeated form or design

❿ 세 자리 수: a three-__________ number

Study Date: ______ / ______

B 다음 [보기]에서 알맞은 말을 골라 문장을 완성하시오.

보기 divide sum calculate suppose add

1 The ________ of 2, 4, and 6 is 12.

2 If you ________ 10 by 5, you will get 2.

3 If you ________ 10 and 5, you will get 15.

4 Tom does not answer the phone, so I ________ he is busy.

5 We are trying to ________ how long the project will take.

생각을 키우는 서술형 • 수행평가 대비 훈련

C 다음 [보기]에서 알맞은 말을 골라 글을 완성하시오.

You can use a calculator and ________ easily. However, people have developed ways to do the job by hand. For example, you can use the multiplication table. It takes some time to ________ the table, but it is very handy. Ancient Egyptians used another ________. It allows you to easily multiply even double-________ numbers. If you learn it, you will ________ that math can be fun.

보기 notice memorize multiply digit method

UNIT 14 Heal the World

생각의 폭을 넓히는 배경지식 Story

#*Topic* Saving the Children

세이브더칠드런(Save the Children)은 비영리 independent organization으로, 1919년 영국에서 설립된 이래, 전 세계의 빈곤 아동을 돕고 있어요. 특히 2007년부터 아프리카 신생아들을 위한 모자 뜨기 캠페인을 시작한 것으로 유명해요. 아프리카에서는 newborn 아이들이 태어난 지 한 달도 되지 않아 저체온증 등으로 목숨을 잃는 경우가 많대요. 특히 아프리카의 밤은 낮과 달리 기온이 상당히 떨어지는데, 그러다보니 newborn 아이들이 밤새 추위를 이기지 못하고 사망하는 것이죠. 그래서 모자를 knit해서 보내는 것만으로도 이러한 아이들에게 희망이 될 수 있어요.

또 다른 조직으로는 유니세프(United Nations Children's Fund)가 있어요. 1946년 설립된 UN의 아동 구호 조직이에요. 전 세계의 굶주리는 어린이들을 위한 critical한 구호, 영양 관리, infection 예방을 위한 접종, 식수 문제 및 환경 개선, 기초 교육 등을 conduct하고 있어요. 특히 한국 전쟁 당시 전쟁의 피해를 입은 어린이들에게 구호물자를 공급하기도 했어요. 오늘날 유니세프 한국 위원회는 다른 나라를 지원하는 successful 사례로 기억되고 있어요.

이 외에도 세계에는 많은 independent 단체들이 아이들이나 도움이 필요한 사람들을 위해 애를 쓰고 있어요. 다른 사람을 돕는 방법은 생각보다 쉬워요. 많은 돈을 donate하지 않아도 되죠. 다만, 여러분의 작은 관심만 있다면 세상은 조금씩 따뜻해질 테니까요.

본문 미리보기 QUIZ

1 말라위에서는 3백만 명의 아이들이 [□ 굶주리고 / □ 농사를 짓고] 있다. 114쪽에서 확인

2 손뜨개에 능숙하지 못하면 대신 [□ 1달러 / □ 10달러]를 보내 아이들을 살릴 수 있다. 116쪽에서 확인

독해의 장벽을 깨는 만만한 Vocabulary

Study Date: ____ / ____

□	1	**conduct** [kəndʌ́kt]	동 수행하다	연구를 수행하다	________ a study
□	2	**critical** [krítikəl]	형 위급한	위태로운 순간	a ________ moment
□	3	**donate** [dóuneit]	동 기부하다	돈을 기부하다	________ some money
□	4	**electronic** [ilektrάnik]	형 전자의	전자계산기	an ________ calculator
□	5	**independent** [ìndipéndənt]	형 독립한	독립 단체	an ________ organization
□	6	**infection** [infékʃən]	명 전염, 감염	감염의 위험	the risk of ________
□	7	**knit** [nit]	동 뜨다, 짜다	스웨터를 짜다	________ a sweater
□	8	**mass** [mæs]	명 다량, 다수	사람들 무리	the ________ of people
□	9	**newborn** [njúːbɔ̀ːrn]	형 새로 태어난	새로 태어난 아기	a ________ baby
□	10	**organization** [ɔ̀ːrgənizéiʃən]	명 기구	비영리 단체	a nonprofit ________
□	11	**statistics** [stətístiks]	명 통계	공식 통계	the official ________
□	12	**successful** [səksésfəl]	형 성공적인	성공적인 캠페인	a ________ campaign
□	13	**survey** [sə́ːrvei]	명 설문 조사	최근의 설문 조사	a recent ________
□	14	**university** [jùːnəvə́ːrsəti]	명 (종합) 대학교	대학 과정	a ________ course
□	15	**within** [wiðín]	전 ~안에	이틀 안에	________ two days

어휘 자신만만 QUIZ

1 반면에 그들은 평균 10달러를 기부할 것이다.

On the other hand, they will ________ an average of ten dollars.

2 거의 4백만 명의 아기들이 태어난 지 한 달 이내에 목숨을 잃는다.

Nearly 4 million babies lose their lives ________ a month after birth.

Reading 01 If I Look at the One

My Reading Time | Words 175 / 1분 55초

1회 ____분 ____초 2회 ____분 ____초

Mother Teresa once said, "If I look at the mass, I will never act. If I look at the one, I will." She meant that willingness to help others begins with one person. Some researchers wanted to test this idea, so in 2007 they conducted a study.

5 A total of 121 students at an American university were asked to fill out a short survey in exchange for $5. The survey was about their use of different electronic products. After completing the survey, each student was given $5 and a letter. They were asked to read the letter carefully before going home. They could donate money if they wanted.

10 The letter was in two different forms. One showed statistics: 3 million hungry children in Malawi and 11 million hungry children in Ethiopia. The other only showed stories about Rokia, a poor and hungry girl from Mali, Africa. The results were very different. People who received the __________ donated an average of $1.17. On the other hand, people who learned about

15 Rokia donated an average of $2.83.

Words

mass 명 다량, 다수 willingness 명 기꺼이 하는 마음 researcher 명 연구자 conduct 동 수행하다 survey 명 설문 조사 in exchange for ~과 교환하여 electronic product 전자 제품 complete 동 완성하다 donate 동 기부하다 statistics 명 통계 million 명 백만 on the other hand 반면에

LINK 실력 향상 WORKBOOK p.54

Main Idea

1 What is the main idea of the passage?

a. People donate more when they earn more money.

b. We should help the hungry children around the world.

c. Mother Teresa was one of the greatest people in the world.

d. People help others more when they hear the story of one person.

Inference

2 빈칸에 들어갈 말로 가장 알맞은 것은?

a. money b. product c. statistics d. stories

Details

3 본문에 소개된 연구에 관한 진술로 옳은 것은?

a. The students filled out a survey about donation.

b. Each student was given $5 after the survey.

c. Each student read two letters.

d. Every student donated some of the money.

Graphic Organizer

4 본문의 단어를 이용하여 표를 완성하시오.

The Process of the Survey	
After filling out a survey, each student received ________ and a letter.	
Read ________ about hungry children in Africa	Read stories about a poor and hungry girl, ________
Donated an average of $1.17	Donated an average of ________
Conclusion	
Willingness to help others begins with the story of ________ ________.	

지식 백과

테레사 수녀(Mother Teresa)

테레사 수녀(1910~1997)는 인도의 로마 가톨릭교회 수녀로, 본명은 Anjeze Gonxhe Bojaxhiu이다. 1950년에 인도의 콜카타에서 '사랑의 선교 수녀회'라는 비정부기구를 설립하였고, 이후 45년간 이 기구를 통해 빈민, 병자, 고아들을 위해 인도 등에서 헌신하였다. 1979년 노벨 평화상을 수상하였고, 2016년 9월 4일 성인으로 추대되었다.

테레사 수녀에 대해 동영상으로 좀 더 알아보세요. Time 2' 24''

Reading 02

Knit One, Save One

My Reading Time | Words 191 / 2분 05초

1회 ____분____초 2회 ____분____초

Most people think that it is hot in Africa. But even in Africa, keeping a newborn baby warm during the first critical days is very important. Every year nearly 4 million babies in Africa lose their lives within a month after birth. Simply putting a little cap on a baby's head can save its life.

5 (A) Save the Children, an independent organization for helping children, started its "Knit One, Save One" campaign in 2007. (B) It was successful in several countries, such as Germany, the U.S., the U.K., and South Korea. (C) For example, 25,000 knitted caps were collected in South 10 Korea in the first year. (D) In the next year, the number reached more than 80,000.

If you are not good at knitting, you can save babies by sending $10. With ten dollars, you can provide a handmade cap and soap for handwashing. The soap will help keep the baby free of infections. Babies 15 are the same all across the world, and each baby has the right to have a healthy start. Remember, just a small donation can save a baby's life.

Words

newborn 형 새로 태어난 critical 형 위급한 within 전 ~안에 independent 형 독립한 organization 명 기구 knit 동 뜨다, 짜다 campaign 명 캠페인, 사회 운동 handmade 형 손으로 만든 soap 명 비누 infection 명 전염, 감염 donation 명 기부

LINK 실력 향상 WORKBOOK p.56

1

Purpose

글을 쓴 목적으로 가장 알맞은 것은?

a. to advertise caps for newborn babies

b. to ask people to give a helping hand

c. to explain how "Knit One, Save One" started

d. to give information about poor children in Africa

2

Organization

주어진 문장이 들어가기에 가장 알맞은 곳은?

The campaign asked people to knit a cap for newborn African babies.

a. (A) b. (B) c. (C) d. (D)

3

Details

문장을 읽고 본문의 내용과 일치하면 T, 일치하지 않으면 F를 쓰시오.

(1) ______ Newborn babies in Africa need to be kept warm.

(2) ______ "Knit One, Save One" is an organization for helping children.

(3) ______ In 2007, 25,000 knitted caps were collected in South Korea.

4

Summary

Complete the summary with the words from the passage.

Providing little caps for ________ babies in Africa can save many lives. Save the Children started the "Knit One, Save One" campaign in ________. The campaign asks people to knit a ________ for newborn babies in Africa. People can donate ________ instead of knitting. Handmade caps and ________ will be provided for newborn babies in Africa.

지식 백과

Save the Children

Save the Children은 전 세계의 빈곤 아동을 돕는 세계 최대의 비영리 국제기구 중 하나이다. 1919년 영국에서 Eglantyne Jebb과 Dorothy Buxton에 의해 설립되었으며, 교육과 보건, 경제적 지원을 통해 아동의 권리를 보호하는 데 목적을 두고 있다. 현재 29개국 이상에 지사를 두고 있으며, 120여 개국 이상에서 활동하고 있다. 국가 간 전쟁이나 재난 등이 일어날 경우에 응급 구호 팀을 파견하기도 한다.

Reading Closer

독해의 내공을 키우는 **마무리 학습**

A Unit 14에서 학습한 단어를 생각해 보고, 다음 퍼즐을 완성해 보시오.

					⑥ n										
							⑦								
① m			⑧		②										
	⑨														
③	n												⑩		
												④ s			
							⑤ c								

Across

① "If I look at the ________, I will never act. If I look at the one, I will."

② 한 달 안에: ________ one month

③ What ________ do you want to enter? (너는 어떤 대학교에 가고 싶니?)

④ a thing that is used for washing

⑤ We will ________ a study on the product.
(우리는 그 제품에 관하여 연구를 수행할 것이다.)

Down

⑥ recently born

⑦ 통계; 통계학

⑧ 최근 조사에 따르면: according to a recent ________

⑨ 뜨개질하는 방법: how to ________

⑩ to give something in order to help a person or organization

Study Date: ____ / ____

B 다음 [보기]에서 알맞은 말을 골라 문장을 완성하시오.

보기	average	critical	collect	infection	complete

1 The project is now at a __________ stage.

2 My parents __________ coins and stamps as a hobby.

3 You should take medicine if you have an ear __________.

4 Students were asked to __________ a survey about allowance.

5 If you add two numbers and divide the total by 2, you will get the __________.

생각을 키우는 서술형 • 수행평가 대비 훈련

C 다음 네모 안에서 알맞은 말을 골라 글을 완성하시오.

Mother Teresa knew that [willingness / ability] to help others begins with one person. In fact, research suggests that people [earn / donate] more when they hear the story of one person in need. Of course, many people help others when they hear about big [statistics / problems] of the needy. For example, people [buy / knit] caps because they know almost 4 million babies in Africa [lose / save] their lives shortly after birth.

UNIT 15 Great Mayans

생각의 폭을 넓히는 배경지식 Story

#Topic Ancient Maya Civilization

아메리카 대륙에서 부흥했던 civilization으로는 마야, 아즈텍, 잉카 문명이 있지만 그 자세한 내용은 밝혀진 것이 많지 않아요. 마야 문명은 현재의 멕시코 동남부에서부터 과테말라, 벨리즈, 엘살바도르 북부, 온두라스 서부 지역에 걸쳐 번영했다고 해요.

Maya civilization은 옥수수를 주식으로 삼은 농업을 중요하게 여겼어요. 농업이 발달하려면 달력이 꼭 필요했죠. 그래서 마야인들은 하늘의 움직임을 살피는 것이 중요하다는 것을 aware했기 때문에 astronomy도 발달했죠. advanced한 천문학을 바탕으로 마야인들은 독자적인 calendar를 만들었어요. 그들은 신께 worship하기 위해 만든 260일 period의 제례력과 지구의 공전 주기를 근거로 365일 period의 긴 주기력도 갖게 되었어요.

마야력은 기원전 3114년 8월 13일을 원년으로 시작하여, 달력의 마지막 날이 기원후 2012년 12월 21일에 멈춰 있어요. 그래서 한 때 2012년 지구 종말론이라는 작은 소동이 있기도 했어요. 실제로는 그냥 2012년에 한 주기가 끝난 것에 불과했거든요. 만약 마야 문명이 망하지 않고 더 지속되었다면 2012년 이후의 달력도 나왔겠죠?

마야 문명은 수학도 발달해 있었어요. 특히 0을 사용했으며, 20진법으로 수를 나타냈다고 해요. 그들은 조개 shell 모양의 타원형은 0, 점은 1, 선은 5를 represent한다고 하네요. 자, 그러면 마야의 문명에 대해 좀 더 알아보는 시간을 가져 볼까요?

본문 미리보기 QUIZ

1 멕시코의 피라미드는 꼭대기가 [□ 뾰족한 / □ 편평한] 모양이다. 122쪽에서 확인

2 그레고리안력(Gregorian calendar)은 [□ 10세기 / □ 16세기] 부터 사용되었다. 124쪽에서 확인

Study Date: ____ / ____

☐ 1	**accurately** [ǽkjurətli]	부 정확하게	매우 정확하게	very ________
☐ 2	**advanced** [ədvǽnst]	형 진보한	진보한 기술	________ technology
☐ 3	**astronomy** [əstránəmi]	명 천문학	현대의 천문학	modern ________
☐ 4	**aware** [əwɛ́ər]	형 인식하는	그것을 인식하다	be ________ of it
☐ 5	**calendar** [kǽləndər]	명 달력	탁상 달력	a desk ________
☐ 6	**civilization** [sìvəlizéiʃən]	명 문명	마야 문명	Maya ________
☐ 7	**concept** [kánsept]	명 개념	0의 개념	the ________ of zero
☐ 8	**consist of**	구성되다	두 부분으로 구성되다	________ of two parts
☐ 9	**narrow** [nǽrou]	형 좁은	좁은 통로	a ________ passage
☐ 10	**period** [píːəriəd]	명 주기, 기간	짧은 기간	a short ________
☐ 11	**represent** [rèprizént]	동 나타내다	그 수를 나타내다	________ the number
☐ 12	**shell** [ʃel]	명 껍질	달팽이의 껍질	a snail ________
☐ 13	**slightly** [sláitli]	부 약간	약간 다르다	be ________ different
☐ 14	**vertically** [vəːrtikəli]	부 수직으로	세로로 선을 긋다	draw a line ________
☐ 15	**worship** [wəːrʃip]	동 숭배하다	신을 숭배하다	________ the god

어휘 자신만만 QUIZ

1 좁은 통로가 그 방을 꼭대기와 연결한다.

A ________ passage connects the room to the top.

2 0의 개념은 수학에서 중심적인 역할을 한다.

The ________ of zero plays a central role in mathematics.

Reading 01

Pyramids in Mexico and Egypt

My Reading Time | Words 185 / 2분 05초

1회 ____분 ____초 2회 ____분 ____초

Almost everyone knows that there are a lot of pyramids in Egypt. Not many people know, however, that the ancient people of Mexico also built great pyramids. The pyramids in Mexico are also large and wonderful. Thousands of people worked for many years to build them, and they did so without modern technology.

The Mexican pyramids are different from the Egyptian ones in shape and structure. An Egyptian pyramid has a pointed top and a small room inside. A narrow passage connects the room to the top of the pyramid. A Mexican pyramid, however, has a flat top and steps which lead to the top.

In addition, the pyramids had different purposes. An Egyptian pyramid was built to help the pharaoh to live forever. The mummy of a pharaoh was laid inside the small room. Ancient Egyptians believed that the pharaoh's soul could travel to heaven through the narrow passage.

__________, a Mexican pyramid was built to worship gods. Ancient Mexicans walked up to the flat top and offered animal and human blood. They believed that their gods needed blood for food.

Words

pyramid 명 피라미드 thousands of 수천의 shape 명 형태 structure 명 구조 pointed 형 뾰족한 narrow 형 좁은 flat 형 편평한 lead to ~으로 이어지다 purpose 명 목적 mummy 명 미라 pharaoh 명 왕, 파라오 worship 동 예배하다 offer 동 제공하다

Study Date: ______ / ______

LINK 실력 향상 WORKBOOK p.58

1

Purpose

What is the purpose of the passage?

a. to show the beauty of Mexican pyramids

b. to compare Mexican pyramids with Egyptian ones

c. to teach the history of Mexican and Egyptian pyramids

d. to tell a story about the ancient peoples in Mexico and Egypt

2

Linking

빈칸에 들어갈 말로 가장 알맞은 것은?

a. In addition　　b. Besides

c. On the other hand　　d. For example

3

Details

다음 질문에 대한 답을 완성하시오.

Q: Why did Mexicans offer animal and human blood to their gods?

A: Because they believed that ______________________.

4

Graphic Organizer

본문의 단어를 이용하여 비교표를 완성하시오.

Mexican Pyramids	Similarities	Egyptian Pyramids
Structure • a __________ top • steps leading to the top	Both are large and __________.	**Structure** • a pointed top • a small room • a __________ connecting the room to the top
Purpose • to worship __________		**Purpose** • to help the __________ live forever

지식 백과

피라미드는 세계 어디에나 있다?

피라미드(pyramid)는 넓은 밑면과 하나의 정점으로 모이는 형태라는 공통점을 가진 건축물을 총칭하는 말이다. 흔히 이집트의 피라미드를 연상하지만, 이러한 형태의 건축물은 세계 곳곳에서 발견된다. 마야 문명의 계단식 돌 피라미드, 중국 고대 황제의 무덤, 고구려의 장군총, 보스니아에 있는 거대한 흙 피라미드 등도 모두 피라미드에 해당한다. 고대의 대형 건축물들은 건축기술의 한계 때문에, 높게 짓기 위해서는 윗부분의 무게를 줄여야 했으므로 대부분 피라미드와 같은 모양이 될 수밖에 없었다.

메시코의 피라미드를 동영상으로 감상하세요. Time 2' 35"

Reading 02

The Great Science of Mayans

My Reading Time | Words 176 / 1분 55초

1회 ____분____초 2회 ____분____초

The Maya civilization was in Central America. During its *Classic Period from A.D. 250 to 900, it was one of the most advanced civilizations in the world. It was especially advanced in mathematics and astronomy.

The Maya civilization was one of the earliest civilizations to use zero. The concept of zero plays a central role in mathematics, but most civilizations of the time did not have it. The Maya people, however, used a flat, round shape to represent zero. They used three symbols to count numbers — a shell for zero, a dot for one, and a line for five. The numbers were written vertically. For example, to represent 13, three dots were written side by side with two lines under them.

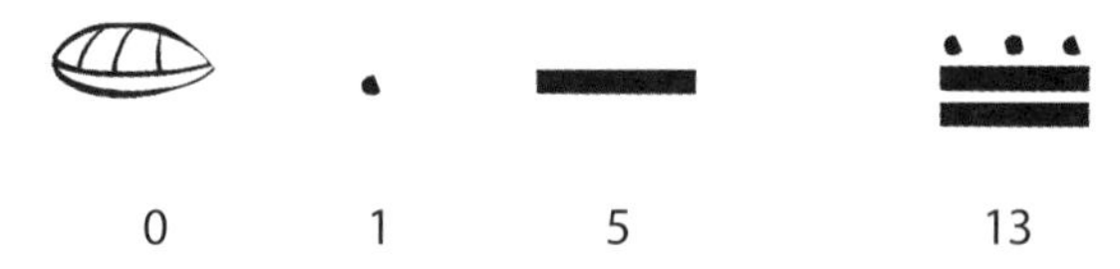

0 1 5 13

The Mayans measured the length of the solar year very accurately. They were aware that a year is a little longer than 365 days. In the Mayan calendar, a year consists of 365.242036 days. This is slightly more accurate than the 365.2425 days of the Gregorian calendar, which has been used since the 16th century.

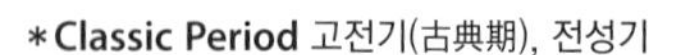

*Classic Period 고전기(古典期), 전성기

Words

civilization 명 문명 period 명 기간 advanced 형 진보한 mathematics 명 수학 astronomy 명 천문학 concept 명 개념 central 형 중심의 shell 명 껍질 vertically 부 수직으로 aware 형 알고 있는 calendar 명 달력 consist of 구성되다 slightly 부 약간

LINK > 실력 향상 WORKBOOK p.60

1 Main Idea

본문이 마야 문명에 대해 주로 설명하는 바로 가장 알맞은 것은?

a. 정확한 달력을 만들었다.

b. 0의 개념을 사용했다.

c. 기호를 이용하여 숫자를 표시했다.

d. 수학과 천문학이 발달되어 있었다.

2 Inference

마야 기호, 가 나타내는 숫자로 가장 알맞은 것은?

a. 6　　b. 10　　c. 15　　d. 18

3 Details

본문의 내용과 일치하지 않는 것은?

a. The Maya civilization existed for about 900 years.

b. A flat, round shape means zero in the Maya civilization.

c. The Mayans knew that the solar year is not exactly 365 days.

d. The Gregorian calendar is used today.

4 Summary

Complete the summary with the words from the passage.

The Maya civilization was advanced in ______________ and astronomy. It was one of the earliest civilizations to use __________, and it had its own number system. A few __________ were used to count numbers. In addition, the Mayans measured the length of the __________ year very accurately.

지식 백과

윤년(leap year)

그레고리안력(Gregorian calendar)은 1582년에 교황 그레고리오 13세(Pope Gregory XIII)가 율리우스력(Julian calendar)을 개정하여 시행했기 때문에 붙여진 이름이다. Julius Caesar가 기원전 46년에 제정한 율리우스력은 4년마다 2월 29일을 추가하는 윤년을 두었는데, 율리우스력의 1년 길이는 365.25일이므로 천문학의 회귀년 365.2422일보다 0.0078일이 길어서 128년마다 1일의 편차가 났다. 그레고리안력은 율리우스력의 매 400년 마다 3번의 윤년을 없애는 방법으로 이를 해결했다.

Reading Closer

독해의 내공을 키우는 **마무리 학습**

A **Unit 15에서 학습한 단어를 생각해 보고, 다음 퍼즐을 완성해 보시오.**

⑦ ②p ③c ⑧ ⑨ ⑩s ④s ⑤ r ⑥ ①

Across

❶ The lion is a ________ of courage. (사자는 용기의 상징이다.)

❷ a very large structure built in ancient Egypt and Mexico

❸ an idea of what something is or how it works

❹ 약간, 조금

❺ long and not wide: small from one side to the other side

Down

❻ the scientific study of stars and planets in outer space

❼ 그 책의 목적: the ________ of the book

❽ located in the center of a thing or place

❾ 기간, 주기

❿ the hard outer covering of an animal, insect, etc.

B 다음 [보기]에서 알맞은 말을 골라 문장을 완성하시오.

보기	civilization	vertically	measure	consist	narrow

1 The car could not pass through the ________ gate.

2 The project team will ________ of five able engineers.

3 Trees grow ________ to get as much sunlight as possible.

4 You should use a good scale to ________ weight exactly.

5 Scientists say that nuclear war would mean the end of ________.

생각을 키우는 서술형 • 수행평가 대비 훈련

C 다음 [보기]에서 알맞은 말을 골라 글을 완성하시오.

Mayans were great in two ways. First, they built large pyramids without much technology. Their pyramids are different from Egyptian ones in ________ and purpose. There are steps that lead to the ________ top, and the pyramids were built to offer ________ to gods. In addition, Mayans were very advanced in mathematics and astronomy. They used the ________ of zero and a very ________ calendar.

보기	accurate	shape	blood	flat	concept

UNIT 16 The Armadillo's Song

생각의 폭을 넓히는 배경지식 Story

#*Topic* Musical Instruments

가을날 풀숲에서는 풀벌레들이 merrily하게 음악을 연주하는 소리를 들을 수 있어요. 특히 cricket은 바이올린 instrument처럼 날개를 비벼 소리를 내요. instrument에 관한 재미있는 이야기가 하나 있어요.

신라시대 신문왕은 아버지인 문무왕을 위해 감은사라는 절을 지었대요. 죽어서도 용이 되어 왜구로부터 나라를 지키겠다고 insist했던 문무왕을 떠올리면서요. 그런데 정말로 문무왕이 용이 되어 나타나, 다음과 같이 말했어요. "너에게 대나무를 줄 것이니, 이것으로 피리를 만들어 불거라. 그러면 온 세상이 평온해질 것이다."

신문왕이 대나무 피리를 만들어 불자 정말 신기하고, ridiculous한 일이 일어났어요. 피리를 불면 적의 군사가 in amazement해서 도망가고, 가뭄에는 비가 내렸으며, 사납게 몰아치던 파도도 평온해졌어요. 그래서 신문왕은 이 피리를 '만파식적(萬波息笛)'이라고 이름 지었어요. '만 개의 파도를 가라앉히는 피리'라는 뜻이죠.

스페인이 잉카 제국을 침략했을 때 몇 가지 서양의 문물도 함께 가지고 왔는데, 그 중에는 기타와 하프 같은 musical instrument도 포함되어 있었죠. 잉카 제국이 망하고, 안데스 지역의 사람들은 오랜 고난의 세월을 견디면서 이들 악기를 자신들에게 맞게 변형시켜 나갔어요. 이렇게 만들어진 악기가 바로 차랑고와 아르파예요. 아르파는 작은 하프로, 음색이 소박하고 우리의 거문고와 비슷한 느낌을 주죠. 차랑고는 기타보다 높은 음을 내는 현악기이고요. 많은 musician들이 이들 악기를 활용해 연주를 한답니다. 자, 이번 시간에는 차랑고에 얽힌 이야기를 함께 읽어 보아요.

본문 미리보기 QUIZ

1 옛날에 음악을 사랑하는 [□ 개구리 / □ 아르마딜로] 한 마리가 있었다. 130쪽에서 확인

2 연못가에서 악기를 연주한 것은 [□ 음악가 / □ 개구리와 아르마딜로] 이다. 132쪽에서 확인

Study Date: ______ / ______

☐ 1	**amazement** [əméizmənt]	명 놀람	놀라서	in ______
☐ 2	**creep** [kri:p]	동 살금살금 걷다	내게 살금살금 오다	______ up on me
☐ 3	**cricket** [kríkit]	명 귀뚜라미	귀뚜라미 소리	the sound of a ______
☐ 4	**desire** [dizáiər]	명 욕구, 바람	승리에 대한 욕구	a ______ for victory
☐ 5	**drag** [dræg]	동 끌고 가다	의자들을 끌다	______ chairs
☐ 6	**insist** [insíst]	동 고집하다	환불을 고집하다	______ on a refund
☐ 7	**instrument** [ínstrəmənt]	명 도구	악기	a musical ______
☐ 8	**merrily** [mérəli]	부 즐겁게	즐겁게 대화하다	talk ______
☐ 9	**musician** [mju:zíʃən]	명 음악가	거리의 음악가	a street ______
☐ 10	**pond** [pɑnd]	명 못, 늪	깊은 연못	a deep ______
☐ 11	**rainfall** [réinfɔ̀:l]	명 강우	적은 강우	low ______
☐ 12	**reluctant** [rilʌ́ktənt]	형 내키지 않는	~을 주저하다	be ______ to
☐ 13	**ridiculous** [ridíkjuləs]	형 터무니없는	우스꽝스럽게 보이다	look ______
☐ 14	**stare** [stɛər]	동 응시하다	나를 응시하다	______ at me
☐ 15	**wizard** [wízərd]	명 마법사	가장 위대한 마법사	the greatest ______

어휘 자신만만 QUIZ

1 아르마딜로는 그의 등딱지를 큰 연못으로 끌어가곤 했다.

The armadillo would ______________ his shell to the large pond.

2 그들은 커다란 눈으로 그를 응시하곤 했다.

They would ______________ at him with big eyes.

Reading 01

How I Wish I Could Sing

My Reading Time | Words 176 / 1분 55초

1회 ____분 ____초 2회 ____분 ____초

There once lived an armadillo who loved music more than anything else in the world. After every rainfall, the armadillo would drag his shell to the large pond. He would listen to the big green frogs singing to each other in the most amazing voices.

"Oh," thought the armadillo, "how I wish I could sing." 5

The frogs were laughing at this funny animal that wanted so badly to sing like a frog.

"Don't be ridiculous," sang the frogs. "Armadillos can't sing."

Then one day a family of crickets moved into a new house near the armadillo. He was amazed to hear them ________ as merrily as the 10 frogs. He would creep next to their house and listen all day and all night for their musical sounds.

"Oh," sighed the armadillo, "how I wish I could sing."

"Don't be ridiculous," sang the crickets. "Armadillos can't sing." 15

Then one day, the armadillo visited the greatest wizard in the area. He said, "Great wizard, it is my deepest desire to learn to sing like the frogs and the crickets." 20

Words armadillo 명 아르마딜로[동물] rainfall 명 강우 drag 동 끌어당기다 pond 명 못, 늪 frog 명 개구리 laugh at 비웃다 ridiculous 형 우스운, 터무니없는 cricket 명 귀뚜라미 merrily 부 즐겁게 creep 동 기다, 살금살금 걷다 wizard 명 마법사 desire 명 욕구, 소망

LINK 실력 향상 WORKBOOK p.62

Main Idea

1 What is the main idea of the story?

a. An armadillo wanted to sing beautifully.

b. An armadillo often heard frogs and crickets sing.

c. An armadillo became a good neighbor to frogs and crickets.

d. An armadillo wished to be a great wizard.

Grammar

2 어법상 빈칸에 들어갈 말로 가장 알맞은 것은?

a. sing　　b. sang

c. to sing　　d. have sung

Details

3 문장을 읽고 본문의 내용과 일치하면 T, 일치하지 않으면 F를 쓰시오.

(1) _____ The armadillo often visited the pond to hear the frogs' songs.

(2) _____ The frogs encouraged the armadillo to sing.

(3) _____ The crickets could sing, but not as well as the frogs.

Making a Prediction

4 본문 다음에는 어떤 일이 일어날까요? 둘 중 하나를 골라 예측을 완성하시오.

☐ The wizard could make the armadillo sing.

____

____

☐ The wizard couldn't make the armadillo sing.

____

____

지식 백과

아르마딜로(armadillo)

포유류 중에서 특이하게 등껍질을 가진 동물이며, 그 이름은 스페인어로 형용사 armado(무장한)와 축소형 어미(-illo)가 합쳐져 armadillo(무장한 조그만 것)에서 유래되었다. 거북의 등딱지와 비슷한 띠 모양의 딱지를 가지고 있으며, 위협을 느끼게 되면 자신의 몸을 말아 포식자로부터 위험을 피할 수 있다. 주로 작은 곤충과 부드러운 식물을 먹고 산다.

아르마딜로에 관해 동영상으로 좀 더 알아보세요. Time 1' 54''

Reading 02

If I Die, I Can Sing

My Reading Time | Words 208 / 2분 12초

1회 ___분 ___초 2회 ___분 ___초

The wizard bent low to the ground and looked the creature in the eye. "I can make you sing, little armadillo," he said. "But ⓐ you do not want to pay the price, for it will mean your ________."

"You mean if I die, I will be able to sing?" asked the armadillo in amazement.

"Yes, this is so," said the wizard.

"Then, ⓑ I want to die right now!" said the armadillo. "I would do anything to be able to sing!"

The wizard was reluctant to take the life of such a fine armadillo. But the creature insisted. Finally, the wizard killed the armadillo, made a musical instrument from ⓒ his shell, and gave it to the finest musician in the town.

Sometimes the musician would play ⓓ his instrument by the pond where the frogs lived. They would stare at him with big eyes and say: "Ai! Ai! The armadillo has learned to sing."

Sometimes the musician would play his instrument by the house where the crickets lived. They would creep outside to stare at him with big eyes and say: "Ai! Ai! The armadillo has learned to sing."

And so it was. The armadillo had learned to sing at last, and his voice was the finest in the land.

Words bend 동 구부리다 creature 명 생물 pay 동 지불하다 price 명 가격 amazement 명 놀람 reluctant 형 꺼리는, 내키지 않는 insist 동 우기다, 고집하다 instrument 명 도구 musician 명 음악가 stare 동 응시하다 at last 마침내

LINK 실력 향상 WORKBOOK p.62

Reference
1 밑줄 친 부분 중 가리키는 바가 나머지와 다른 것은?

a. ⓐ b. ⓑ c. ⓒ d. ⓓ

Words
2 빈칸에 들어갈 말로 가장 알맞은 것은?

a. sadness
b. death
c. money
d. misfortune

Details
3 다음 중 본문의 내용과 일치하지 않는 것은?

a. The wizard was happy to take the armadillo's life.
b. The armadillo wanted to sing no matter what it costs.
c. A musical instrument was made from the armadillo's shell.
d. The frogs and the crickets were surprised to hear the armadillo sing.

Summary
4 **Complete the summary with the words from the story.**

There lived a fine armadillo. The armadillo wished he could sing as well as __________ or crickets. One day, he visited a great __________ and asked him how he could learn to sing. The wizard killed the armadillo and made a musical instrument from his __________. The finest __________ in the town sometimes played the instrument. The armadillo had learned to __________ at last.

지식백과

차랑고(charango)

안데스 지방의 전통 악기 차랑고는 줄이 10개인 현악기로 원래 아르마딜로 가죽으로 만들었다. 남미 안데스 지방의 인디오들이 아르마딜로 가죽으로 45~60 cm 정도 길이가 되는 소형 현악기를 만들었으며, 잉카 음악의 연주에 없어서는 안 되는 악기가 되었다. 하지만 무분별한 남획으로 멸종 위기에 처하면서 아르마딜로는 보호종으로 관리되고 있으며, 요즘 차랑고는 아르마딜로 가죽 대신에 나무로 제작되고 있다.

Reading Closer

독해의 내공을 키우는 **마무리 학습**

A Unit 16에서 학습한 단어를 생각해 보고, 다음 퍼즐을 완성해 보시오.

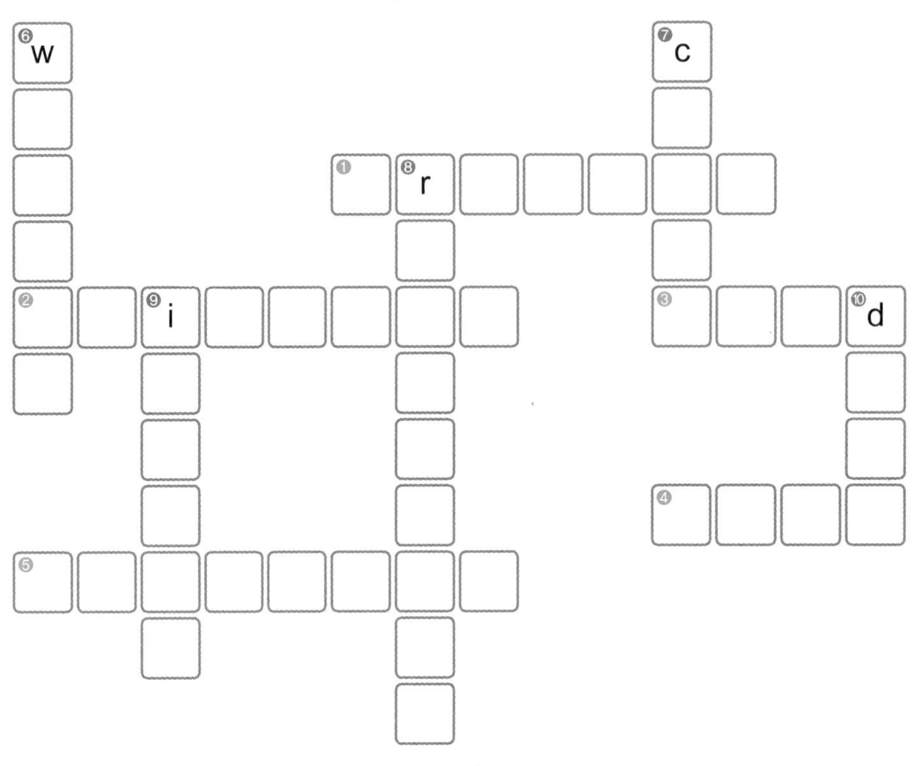

Across

❶ 귀뚜라미

❷ 강우량을 측정하다: measure the ________

❸ an area of water that is smaller than a lake

❹ a small jumping animal, without a tail, that lives on land and in water

❺ a person who writes, sings, or plays music

Down

❻ a person who is skilled in magic or who has magical powers

❼ 기다; 슬금슬금 조용히 다가오다

❽ 마음 내키지 않는, 마지못해 하는

❾ If you ________ upon it, I won't come here again.
(당신이 그것을 고집한다면, 나는 여기에 다시 오지 않을 것이다.)

❿ to draw or pull someone or something that is difficult to move

B 다음 [보기]에서 알맞은 말을 골라 문장을 완성하시오.

보기	creature	price	stare	ridiculous	amazing

1 The man looked so ________ that everyone laughed.

2 It is not polite to ________ at a stranger for a long time.

3 The movie is about a strange ________ from outer space.

4 This pill is ________; it helped me get better in just ten minutes.

5 Drivers are worried that the ________ of gasoline would go up soon.

생각을 키우는 서술형 • 수행평가 대비 훈련

C 다음 네모 안에서 알맞은 말을 골라 글을 완성하시오.

I read a story about an armadillo who lived by a [pond / river]. The armadillo was unhappy because he could not sing as [quickly / merrily] as his animal friends. When he visited a great [animal / wizard], I thought that he would help him. However, he killed the armadillo and made an [instrument / error] with his shell. The finest musician in the town played it, and the animals heard the armadillo's beautiful [voice / name]. I wonder what kind of song the dead armadillo sang.

Make Your Own Quotes

앞에서 배운 내용 중에서
마음속에 간직하고 싶은
좋은 문장들을 여기에 적어 봅시다!

Everyone is able to make the world a better place. (50쪽)
누구나 세상을 좀 더 나은 곳으로 만들 수 있다.

배움으로 행복한 내일을 꿈꾸는

천재교육 커뮤니티 안내

교재 안내부터 구매까지 한 번에!

천재교육 홈페이지

자사가 발행하는 참고서, 교과서에 대한 소개는 물론
도서 구매도 할 수 있습니다. 회원에게 지급되는 별을 모아
다양한 상품 응모에도 도전해 보세요!

다양한 교육 꿀팁에 깜짝 이벤트는 덤!

천재교육 인스타그램

천재교육의 새롭고 중요한 소식을 가장 먼저 접하고 싶다면?
천재교육 인스타그램 팔로우가 필수!
깜짝 이벤트도 수시로 진행되니 놓치지 마세요!

수업이 편리해지는

천재교육 ACA 사이트

오직 선생님만을 위한, 천재교육 모든 교재에 대한 정보가 담긴
아카 사이트에서는 다양한 수업자료 및 부가 자료는 물론
시험 출제에 필요한 문제도 다운로드하실 수 있습니다.

https://aca.chunjae.co.kr

천재교육을 사랑하는 샘들의 모임

천사샘

학원 강사, 공부방 선생님이시라면 누구나 가입할 수 있는 천사샘!
교재 개발 및 평가를 통해 교재 검토진으로 참여할 수 있는 기회는 물론
다양한 교사용 교재 증정 이벤트가 선생님을 기다립니다.

아이와 함께 성장하는 학부모들의 모임공간

튠맘 학습연구소

튠맘 학습연구소는 초·중등 학부모를 대상으로 다양한 이벤트와 함께
교재 리뷰 및 학습 정보를 제공하는 네이버 카페입니다.
초등학생, 중학생 자녀를 둔 학부모님이라면 튠맘 학습연구소로 오세요!

바로 읽는 독해

배경 지식

LEVEL

2

WORKBOOK

CHUNJAE
EDUCATION, INC.

바로 읽는 독해

배경 지식

WORKBOOK

바로 읽는 배경지식 독해

실력 향상 WORKBOOK

LEVEL 2

01 Scotland Saved by Thistles

쉬운 독해를 위한 Vocabulary 업그레이드

A

다음 영어 표현을 읽고 뜻을 쓰시오.

1 plant ____________
2 thick ____________
3 quickly ____________
4 hurt ____________
5 attack ____________
6 surround ____________
7 castle ____________
8 moat ____________
9 pain ____________
10 steal ____________
11 take off ____________
12 defeat ____________
13 save ____________
14 loudly ____________
15 suddenly ____________
16 fast asleep ____________

B

다음 주어진 표현을 배열하여 우리말을 영어로 쓰시오.

1 사실, 그것은 스코틀랜드를 구하는 데 큰 역할을 했다.
(Scotland / fact / it / in / played / saving / in / a big role)

2 그 이야기는 몇 백 년 전으로 거슬러 올라간다.
(back / hundreds / ago / the story / to / of / goes / years)

3 바이킹족은 그 성에 닿기 위해 해자를 그냥 헤엄쳐서 가로질러 갔다.
(the castle / just swam / across / the Vikings / the moat / to / get to)

4 그 고통의 비명은 스코틀랜드 사람들을 깨웠다.
(woke / of / the cries / the Scottish / pain)

끊어 읽기 구문 학습으로 독해 실력 업그레이드

Study Date: /

C

다음과 같이 끊어진 표시에 유의하여 읽고, 문장을 우리말로 해석하시오.

1 The thistle / is / a plant / that / is covered with / small needles.

2 If / you / touch / the thistle / with your hand, / it / will really hurt.

3 Thistles / grow / in thick groups / and cover / an area / quickly.

4 How did / such a plant / become / the national flower / of Scotland?

5 At that time, / the Vikings / attacked / many different countries.

6 Most castles / were surrounded by / a deep trench / called "moat."

7 One night / the Vikings / came to / the Scottish king's castle.

8 The Vikings / took off / their shoes / and jumped into / the moat.

9 Suddenly, / they / began to cry out / loudly. // The moat / was full of / thistles.

10 They / were able to / defeat / the Vikings.

02 Thistles: Harmful or Useful?

쉬운 독해를 위한 Vocabulary 업그레이드

A

다음 영어 표현을 읽고 뜻을 쓰시오.

1 sharp ______________

2 purple ______________

3 consider ______________

4 harmful ______________

5 farmer ______________

6 remove ______________

7 medicine ______________

8 useful ______________

9 prevent ______________

10 repair ______________

11 damage ______________

12 blood ______________

13 waste ______________

14 toxin ______________

15 seed ______________

16 growth ______________

B

다음 주어진 표현을 배열하여 우리말을 영어로 쓰시오.

1 엉겅퀴는 종종 농부들에 의해 해롭다고 여겨진다.
(a thistle / often considered / by / harmful / is / farmers)

2 일단 심어지면, 그것은 대지의 넓은 면적을 빠르게 덮는다.
(it / planted / once / is / it / area / of / quickly / a large / the land / covers)

3 큰엉겅퀴는 간의 손상을 예방하고 치료하는 데 좋다.
(milk thistle / preventing / is good / for / liver / and repairing / damage)

4 그것은 혈액에 있는 찌꺼기와 독소를 제거한다.
(removes / and toxins / it / from / waste / the blood)

끊어 읽기 구문 학습으로 독해 실력 업그레이드

Study Date: ______ / ______

C

다음과 같이 끊어진 표시에 유의하여 읽고, 문장을 우리말로 해석하시오.

1 Thistle / is / the name of plants / with sharp leaves / and purple flowers.

2 It / grows / quickly, / and it / kills / other plants.

3 In Australia, / there was / even a law / that people / had to remove / it / from their land.

4 But / for medicine, / thistle / is / very useful.

5 Their use / as medicine / dates back to / the 4th century B.C.

6 Among the many kinds / which / have a medical effect, / milk thistle / is / the most famous / and important.

7 The liver / is like / a filter / for the blood.

8 Silymarin, / which / is / in milk thistle seeds, / can repair / damaged liver cells.

9 Milk thistle / can also lower / cholesterol levels.

10 Some people / say / that / it / can slow / the growth of cancer cells, / but scientists / are / not sure yet.

01 Addicted to Cell Phones

쉬운 독해를 위한 Vocabulary 업그레이드

A

다음 영어 표현을 읽고 뜻을 쓰시오.

1 upset ______________

2 sweat ______________

3 without ______________

4 recent ______________

5 addicted ______________

6 positive ______________

7 contact ______________

8 reason ______________

9 a lot ______________

10 study ______________

11 effect ______________

12 everywhere ______________

13 part ______________

14 take a break ______________

15 all sorts of ______________

16 break out ______________

B

다음 주어진 표현을 배열하여 우리말을 영어로 쓰시오.

1 휴대 전화 배터리가 다 닳으면, 당신은 식은땀이 나는가?
(do you / break / sweat / when / your cell phone / out / in a cold / battery / dies?)

2 최근 한 연구는 몇몇 사람들이 휴대 전화에 중독되었을 수 있다는 것을 발견했다. (a recent / addicted to / their / some people / could be / study / found that / cell phones)

3 그것은 전화를 끊는 좋은 이유가 될지도 모른다!
(a good / hang / reason / to / up / that / might / be / the phone!)

4 그들은 스트레스를 덜 느꼈다. (felt / stressed / less / they)

끊어 읽기 구문 학습으로 독해 실력 업그레이드

Study Date: ____ / ____

C

다음과 같이 끊어진 표시에 유의하여 읽고, 문장을 우리말로 해석하시오.

1 Will / you / be upset / if / you / cannot use / your cell phone / at school?

2 If / you / can't live / without your cell phone, / you / might have / a problem.

3 About 40 percent of students / said / they / couldn't live / without their cell phones.

4 About 90 percent / said / they / took / their phones / with them / everywhere.

5 The study / shows / that / students / use / their / phones / a lot.

6 This / has / some positive effects / such as / staying in contact / with friends.

7 But / sending / all those text messages / or / doing / all sorts of things online / costs / time and money.

8 As part of the study, / some students / agreed / to take / a break / from their cell phones.

9 After three phone-free days, / students / said / that they felt freer / than before.

02 Cell Phones: How Smart!

쉬운 독해를 위한 Vocabulary 업그레이드

A

다음 영어 표현을 읽고 뜻을 쓰시오.

1 luxury ______________

2 imagine ______________

3 brick ______________

4 function ______________

5 receive ______________

6 record ______________

7 connect ______________

8 communicate ______________

9 tiny ______________

10 of course ______________

11 regard ______________

12 tool ______________

13 entertainment ______________

14 source ______________

15 pay ______________

16 average ______________

B

다음 주어진 표현을 배열하여 우리말을 영어로 쓰시오.

1 휴대 전화는 우리가 서로 대화하는 방법을 변화시켜 왔다.
(have changed / the way / each / other / we / cell phones / talk to)

2 우리는 문자 메시지로 의사소통을 할 수 있다.
(can / messages / communicate / text / with / we)

3 초기의 휴대 전화는 오늘날의 전화기보다 훨씬 더 컸다.
(early / bigger / today's phones / than / cell phones / were / much)

4 그들은 휴대 전화 없이 살 수 없다고 느낀다.
(they / without / they cannot / live / feel / them)

끊어 읽기 구문 학습으로 독해 실력 업그레이드

Study Date: /

C

다음과 같이 끊어진 표시에 유의하여 읽고, 문장을 우리말로 해석하시오.

1 Not so long ago, / cell phones / were / a luxury, / not a necessity.

2 It / is / hard to imagine now, / but / in the early 1990s / the average cell phone / was / as big as a brick / and / only had one function: / to make and receive calls.

3 We / can also take / photos / and / share / them / with other people.

4 Cell phone makers / are adding / new functions / every day.

5 We / can exchange / e-mail, play games, watch movies, record events, pay for bus rides, and connect / with others / using a social networking service.

6 Of course, / we / can still talk / on them. // All of this / is / in one tiny box.

7 People of nearly all ages / have really started / to think of cell phones / in different ways.

8 They / regard / cell phones / not only as a communication tool, / but also as an important source of entertainment.

01 Whose Shadow Is It?

쉬운 독해를 위한 Vocabulary 업그레이드

A

다음 영어 표현을 읽고 뜻을 쓰시오.

1 greedy ____________

2 village ____________

3 shade ____________

4 sunset ____________

5 yard ____________

6 original ____________

7 shadow ____________

8 inside ____________

9 pass by ____________

10 leave ____________

11 price ____________

12 angry ____________

13 sell ____________

14 decide ____________

15 lie (과거형 lay) ____________

16 belong to ____________

B

다음 주어진 표현을 배열하여 우리말을 영어로 쓰시오.

1 그 남자는 그 소년이 그것을 하도록 하지 않았다.
(the man / the boy / do / that / did not / let)

2 그 소년은 화가 났고 뭔가 하기로 마음먹었다.
(decided / angry / and / to / do / something / the boy / got)

3 그는 남자에게 그늘을 자신에게 팔라고 청했다.
(the man / to / he / asked / to him / sell / the shadow)

4 그는 원래 가격의 세 배를 소년에게 지불해야 했다.
(to / pay / the boy / price / he / had / three / times / the original)

끊어 읽기 구문 학습으로 독해 실력 업그레이드

Study Date: /

C

다음과 같이 끊어진 표시에 유의하여 읽고, 문장을 우리말로 해석하시오.

1 Once upon a time / there lived / a greedy man / in a small village.

2 On a hot summer day, / a boy / was passing by / the village.

3 The boy / rested / in the shade / of the tree / next to the man's house.

4 When the man / saw / the boy, / he / said, / "Hey, / my grandfather / planted / this tree, / so its shadow / belongs to / me."

5 At sunset, / the shadow of the tree / was / inside the man's yard.

6 The boy / walked in / and lay there.

7 The man / told / the boy / to leave, // but he / answered, / "I / bought / this shadow / from you, / so it / now belongs to me."

8 When the shadow / was / inside the man's room, / the boy / walked in / and lay there.

9 After the boy / repeated / this / for several days, / the man / couldn't stand / it anymore.

10 He / asked / the boy / to sell the shadow / back to him.

02 Light Makes Shadow

쉬운 독해를 위한 Vocabulary 업그레이드

A

다음 영어 표현을 읽고 뜻을 쓰시오.

1 follow ____________________

2 wherever ____________________

3 form ____________________

4 nature ____________________

5 straight ____________________

6 object ____________________

7 opposite ____________________

8 quite ____________________

9 path ____________________

10 around ____________________

11 angle ____________________

12 block ____________________

13 sunlight ____________________

14 at noon ____________________

15 in addition ____________________

16 in contrast ____________________

B

다음 주어진 표현을 배열하여 우리말을 영어로 쓰시오.

1 우리의 그림자는 항상 우리 주위를 따라다니는 친구이다.
(a friend / always follows / who / our shadow / is / us / around)

2 그림자는 그 반대편에 생긴다. (formed / opposite / on the / a shadow / is / side)

3 키가 작은 사람도 긴 그림자를 갖는다. (a long / a short / shadow / has / even / person)

4 이것은 그림자가 그 크기를 바꾸게 만든다. (the shadow / its size / this / to change / causes)

끊어 읽기 구문 학습으로 독해 실력 업그레이드

Study Date: ____ / ____

C

다음과 같이 끊어진 표시에 유의하여 읽고, 문장을 우리말로 해석하시오.

1 When / there is / light, / it / stays / with us / wherever we go.

2 Have / you / ever wondered / how a shadow is formed?

3 The answer / is / in the nature of light. // Light / travels / in a straight line.

4 If / there are / many sources of light, / we / can see / many shadows / around the same object.

5 In addition, / our shadow / is / a friend / who / changes its size.

6 It / can be / very long / or very short.

7 For example, / when / the sun / is rising / in the east, / our shadow / is / quite long.

8 In contrast, / the shadow / is / very short / at noon / when / the sun / is / high in the sky.

9 Even a tall person / has / a short shadow.

10 As / the earth / rotates / during the day, / the sunlight / falls / on us / at different angles.

01 Hot Air Balloon

쉬운 독해를 위한 Vocabulary 업그레이드

A

다음 영어 표현을 읽고 뜻을 쓰시오.

1 principle ______

2 sink ______

3 float ______

4 basket ______

5 passenger ______

6 flame ______

7 fabric ______

8 hot air balloon ______

9 layer ______

10 control ______

11 heat ______

12 direction ______

13 land ______

14 exactly ______

15 produce ______

16 turn around ______

B

다음 주어진 표현을 배열하여 우리말을 영어로 쓰시오.

1 더운 공기는 기구를 밀어 올리고 이것을 계속 떠 있게 한다.
(up / pushes / the balloon / it / and / keeps / the hot air / floating)

2 바구니는 승객들이 타는 곳이다.
(the place / passengers / the basket / is / where / ride)

3 그것은 공기를 데우기 위해 큰 화염을 만들어 낸다.
(the air / flame / it / produces / a big / to / heat)

4 기구가 사실상 공기 중에서 회전할지도 모른다.
(in / actually / turn / may / the air / around / the balloon)

끊어 읽기 구문 학습으로 독해 실력 업그레이드

Study Date: /

C

다음과 같이 끊어진 표시에 유의하여 읽고, 문장을 우리말로 해석하시오.

1 What / keeps / a hot air balloon / in the sky?

2 A hot air balloon / has / three parts: / the basket, the burner, and the envelope.

3 The burner / is / above / the passengers' heads.

4 The envelope / is / the colorful fabric bag / that holds / the hot air.

5 When the air inside the envelope / is / heated, / the balloon / rises.

6 Once in the air, / the balloon / just floats / with the wind.

7 The pilot / doesn't know exactly / where the balloon / will / land.

8 However, / he or she / can control / the landing / by using / different layers of air.

9 The pilot / can move / the balloon / up or down / by controlling / the heat / in the envelope.

10 Often / the pilot / can / find / a layer of air / that will allow / the balloon / to change direction.

02 Enjoy Hot Air Ballooning

쉬운 독해를 위한 Vocabulary 업그레이드

A

다음 영어 표현을 읽고 뜻을 쓰시오.

1 excellent ______________

2 experience ______________

3 safety ______________

4 record ______________

5 still ______________

6 temperature ______________

7 unstable ______________

8 remember ______________

9 glide ______________

10 provide ______________

11 recommend ______________

12 relaxed ______________

13 ride ______________

14 silently ______________

15 company ______________

16 strongly ______________

B

다음 주어진 표현을 배열하여 우리말을 영어로 쓰시오.

1 낮 동안에는 온도가 올라간다. (the temperature / the day, / during / goes / up)

2 따뜻한 옷을 강력히 권장한다. (are / recommended / strongly / warm / clothes)

3 공기 중의 온도는 종종 지상보다도 더 낮다.
(the air / is / lower / often / the ground / the / on / than / temperature / in)

4 비행을 예약하기 전에, 먼저 그 회사의 안전 기록과 조종사의 경력을 확인해라. (before / safety record / a flight, / and the pilot's / the company's / booking / first check out / experience)

끊어 읽기 구문 학습으로 독해 실력 업그레이드

Study Date: /

C

다음과 같이 끊어진 표시에 유의하여 읽고, 문장을 우리말로 해석하시오.

1 Hot air ballooning / is probably / the slowest way / to fly, / but it / is / one of the most exciting sports / to enjoy.

2 These days, / many hot air balloon companies / provide / excellent, safe flying experiences.

3 There are / a few tips / for enjoying / a hot air balloon ride, / though.

4 You / can visit / the company's website / for all this information.

5 It / is / a good idea / to ride a hot air balloon / in the early morning / or in the evening / because the air / is still / at these times.

6 Since / hot air / rises, / the balloon / can be / unstable.

7 Also, you / need to remember / it / can be / quite cold up / in the sky.

8 Once / in the air, / you / will glide / silently across / the sky.

9 As you / look down at / all the busy people below, / you / may feel / both excited and relaxed.

10 Start / saving for / a hot air balloon ride / now!

01 Just One Dollar

쉬운 독해를 위한 Vocabulary 업그레이드

A

다음 영어 표현을 읽고 뜻을 쓰시오.

1 pay ____________

2 ideal ____________

3 different ____________

4 college ____________

5 physics ____________

6 killer ____________

7 direct ____________

8 nightmare ____________

9 finally ____________

10 interest ____________

11 screenplay ____________

12 go for it ____________

13 what if ____________

14 movie director ____________

15 come true ____________

16 a box office hit ____________

B

다음 주어진 표현을 배열하여 우리말을 영어로 쓰시오.

1 만약 그 직업이 당신의 이상적인 직업이라면 어떨까? (it / were / what / ideal / if / your / job?)

2 여전히, 많은 사람들이 그 직업을 택하려 하지 않을 것이다.
(people / for / it / would / still, / most / not / go)

3 대학에서 그는 물리학을 전공하고 독학으로 특수 효과에 대해 배웠다. (effects / on his / studied / in / about / physics / and learned / college, / he / special / own)

4 어느 날 그는 살인 로봇에 대한 악몽을 꾸었다.
(had / a nightmare / one / a killer / day / he / about / robot)

끊어 읽기 구문 학습으로 독해 실력 업그레이드

Study Date: /

C

다음과 같이 끊어진 표시에 유의하여 읽고, 문장을 우리말로 해석하시오.

1 Would you / take / a job / if it / paid / just one dollar?

2 James Cameron, / the movie director / of Avatar, / was different.

3 He / always dreamed about / becoming a movie director / someday.

4 The robot / was sent / from the future / to kill him.

5 The dream / gave / him / the idea for The Terminator, / and he / wrote / a screenplay / for the movie / in 1984.

6 He / badly wanted / to direct / his own movie.

7 Many companies / showed / interest / in the screenplay, / but they / wouldn't let / Cameron / direct it.

8 Finally, / Cameron / found / a company, / Hemdale Pictures.

9 They / bought / the screenplay / for just one dollar / and let / him / direct / the movie.

10 The Terminator / was / a box office hit, / and Cameron / made / his dream / come true.

02 Choosing a Job

쉬운 독해를 위한 Vocabulary 업그레이드

A 다음 영어 표현을 읽고 뜻을 쓰시오.

1 choose ____________

2 decision ____________

3 around ____________

4 spend ____________

5 explore ____________

6 choice ____________

7 information ____________

8 photographer ____________

9 regret ____________

10 gather ____________

11 take a photo ____________

12 set a goal ____________

13 later on ____________

14 make a decision ____________

15 a variety of ____________

16 keep in mind ____________

B 다음 주어진 표현을 배열하여 우리말을 영어로 쓰시오.

1 직업을 선택하는 것은 매우 중요한 결정이다.
(is / a very / decision / important / choosing / a job)

2 당신은 직업을 찾을 때 어느 정도의 시간과 에너지를 쏟아야 한다.
(put / should / into / it / and / some time / energy / you)

3 목표를 설정하고 그것들을 이루기 위해 열심히 노력하라.
(and / try hard / up / goals / achieve / them / to / set)

4 다양한 출처를 통해 그 직업에 대한 정보를 수집하라.
(about / the job / gather / of / from / information / sources / a variety)

끊어 읽기 구문 학습으로 독해 실력 업그레이드

Study Date: /

C

다음과 같이 끊어진 표시에 유의하여 읽고, 문장을 우리말로 해석하시오.

1 How / are / you / going to choose / your ideal job?

2 There are / three important things / you / should keep in mind / when choosing a job.

3 First, remember / that you / are going to work / around 40 hours a week / at your job.

4 This / means / you / will have to choose / a job / that you really like.

5 If you / like to spend / the whole day cooking, / you / will be / a good cook.

6 If you / like to take / photos, / you / might be / a great photographer.

7 You / may even talk / to someone / who has your ideal job.

8 This way, / you / can make / a decision / you won't regret / later on.

9 Just thinking about / an ideal job / won't help / you get it.

10 You / need to have / clear goals / and work / toward them.

01 Ryan's Well

쉬운 독해를 위한 Vocabulary 업그레이드

A

다음 영어 표현을 읽고 뜻을 쓰시오.

1 continue ______________
2 household ______________
3 church ______________
4 dozen ______________
5 success ______________
6 ordinary ______________
7 graduate ______________
8 achievement ______________
9 chores ______________
10 raise ______________
11 so far ______________
12 foundation ______________
13 hundreds of ______________
14 all kinds of ______________
15 those who ______________
16 be unable to ______________

B

다음 주어진 표현을 배열하여 우리말을 영어로 쓰시오.

1 그는 아프리카에 우물을 지을 돈을 모으기로 결심했다.
(decided / to / money / he / wells / in / raise / for building / Africa)

2 그는 첫 번째 70달러를 벌기 위해 넉 달 동안 갖가지 집안일을 했다. (kinds / did / to / he / of / for / chores / household / four months / all / raise / his first $70)

3 그는 2013년에 대학을 졸업했고 지금은 그 재단을 위해 일한다.
(he / the foundation / in 2013 / and now works / from / college / for / graduated)

4 누구나 세상을 좀 더 나은 곳으로 만들 수 있다.
(to / the world / make / a better / is / place / everyone / able)

끊어 읽기 구문 학습으로 독해 실력 업그레이드

Study Date: /

C 다음과 같이 끊어진 표시에 유의하여 읽고, 문장을 우리말로 해석하시오.

1 Ryan Hreljac / learned from / his teacher / that many people in Africa / were dying / because they / did not have / enough clean water.

2 He / wanted / to do something / about the problem.

3 With this money, / his first well / was built / in 1999 / in a village in Uganda.

4 Ryan / was / only seven years old. // Ryan / has continued / to raise money.

5 He / has given / talks / at hundreds of / schools, churches, and events.

6 People / have felt sorry for / those who / are unable to drink / clean water / and have decided / to give a helping hand.

7 So far, / Ryan's Well Foundation / has built / over 1,000 wells / in more than a dozen countries.

8 When someone / asks about / his achievements, / Ryan / says / he is just an ordinary person.

9 As a young boy, / he / loved / playing basketball, ice hockey, and video games.

10 Ryan's success / shows / that ordinary people / can do / incredible things.

02 The Right to Clean Water

쉬운 독해를 위한 Vocabulary 업그레이드

A 다음 영어 표현을 읽고 뜻을 쓰시오.

1 climate ______

2 element ______

3 bathe ______

4 essential ______

5 decrease ______

6 shortage ______

7 improve ______

8 organization ______

9 risk ______

10 disease ______

11 unsafe ______

12 experience ______

13 global ______

14 properly ______

15 instead of ______

16 in short supply ______

B 다음 주어진 표현을 배열하여 우리말을 영어로 쓰시오.

1 물은 우리 생활에 가장 필수적인 요소이다.
(the most / element / water / for / is / essential / life)

2 깨끗한 물이 적게 공급되기 때문에, 사람들은 때때로 안전하지 않은 물을 마셔야만 한다. (clean water / since / in short supply, / is / drink / sometimes have to / people / unsafe water)

3 그것은 콜레라와 장티푸스와 같은 다양한 질병의 위험성을 높인다.
(the risk of / it / increases / various diseases / cholera and typhoid / like)

4 적절하게 목욕을 하거나 자신의 옷을 씻는 것은 쉬운 일이 아니다.
(not easy / it / wash / their clothes / is / to bathe / properly / or)

끊어 읽기 구문 학습으로 독해 실력 업그레이드

Study Date: /

C 다음과 같이 끊어진 표시에 유의하여 읽고, 문장을 우리말로 해석하시오.

1 But in some countries / in the Middle East and North Africa, / many people / don't have / enough water.

2 Because of climate change, / the amount of water / has decreased / in this region.

3 It / also means / they / cannot bathe / or clean / their clothes / properly.

4 In many regions, / girls / have to walk / many miles / from their homes / to get water / instead of going to school.

5 To solve the problem, / organizations / like the World Bank / started / a project.

6 The bank / is helping / several countries / improve / their water supply systems.

7 The bank / is also helping / countries / share / their knowledge and experience.

8 Water shortage / is not / just a problem / in Africa or the Middle East.

9 So the global community / must work together / to make sure / that everyone / has a right / to clean water.

01 How a Flush Toilet Works

쉬운 독해를 위한 Vocabulary 업그레이드

A

다음 영어 표현을 읽고 뜻을 쓰시오.

1 modern ______________
2 invention ______________
3 operation ______________
4 gravity ______________
5 typical ______________
6 replace ______________
7 major ______________
8 ancient ______________
9 toilet ______________
10 tank ______________
11 flush ______________
12 lever ______________
13 allow ______________
14 pipe ______________
15 importance ______________
16 impact ______________

B

다음 주어진 표현을 배열하여 우리말을 영어로 쓰시오.

1 수세식 화장실은 우리의 삶을 더 쉽고 깨끗하게 해주고 있다.
(easier / toilets / have made / and cleaner / flush / our lives)

2 수세식 화장실은 중력 때문에 작동한다.
(works / because / a flush / toilet / of / gravity)

3 이것은 물이 변기를 채우기 위해 흘러 나가게 한다.
(water / to flow out / to / fill / this / allows / the bowl)

4 더러운 물은 빠져 나가고 깨끗한 물로 교체된다.
(goes out / and is / clean water / the dirty / water / replaced / by)

끊어 읽기 구문 학습으로 독해 실력 업그레이드

Study Date: ______ / ______

C

다음과 같이 끊어진 표시에 유의하여 읽고, 문장을 우리말로 해석하시오.

1 These days, / almost every house or building / has / flush toilets.

2 Flush toilets / were first used / in India / about 2,700 years ago.

3 There were / also flush toilets / in ancient Egypt, Persia, and China.

4 While / the designs / may vary, / the basic operation / is / the same.

5 A typical flush toilet / has / a water tank / above its toilet bowl.

6 When / the lever / is pulled, / a plug in the tank / opens.

7 When / the bowl / is / full enough, / gravity / causes / the water / to flow out / through a pipe.

8 The flush toilet / allows / us / to live in much bigger cities.

9 Because / water / cleans / the toilets / very well, / diseases / cannot spread / as easily as in the past.

10 The flush toilet / may at first seem to be / an invention of minor importance, / but its impact / on our modern world / is / huge.

02 Toilet Paper

쉬운 독해를 위한 Vocabulary 업그레이드

A

다음 영어 표현을 읽고 뜻을 쓰시오.

1 wood ____________

2 clay ____________

3 history ____________

4 commonly ____________

5 emperor ____________

6 producer ____________

7 efficient ____________

8 consider ____________

9 stone ____________

10 sensitive ____________

11 convenient ____________

12 embarrassing ____________

13 expensive ____________

14 instead of ____________

15 company ____________

16 a sheet of ____________

B

다음 주어진 표현을 배열하여 우리말을 영어로 쓰시오.

1 과거의 사람들은 화장지를 사용하지 않았다.
(use / toilet / didn't / people in / the past / paper)

2 고대 그리스인은 돌과 점토 조각을 사용했다.
(used / stones / and pieces / the ancient / Greeks / of clay)

3 화장지라는 발상이 그 당시에는 매우 쑥스럽고 민감한 것이었다.
(paper / the / and sensitive / idea of / toilet /was too embarrassing / at that time)

4 그들의 생산품은 우리의 삶을 더욱 편하고 효율적이며 청결하게 해준다.
(our lives / efficient, / and cleaner / more / their products / make / convenient)

끊어 읽기 구문 학습으로 독해 실력 업그레이드

Study Date: /

C

다음과 같이 끊어진 표시에 유의하여 읽고, 문장을 우리말로 해석하시오.

1 Have / you / ever wondered // "When / was / toilet paper / invented?"

2 Instead of toilet paper, / people / used / everything you can imagine / —wood, leaves, water, or snow.

3 People in the Middle East commonly / used / the left hand.

4 So, that hand / is still considered / unclean / in that part of the world.

5 The history of toilet paper / goes back to / the late 14th century / in China.

6 Chinese emperors / used / a large sheet of paper / which was specially produced.

7 Rolled toilet paper / was invented / around 1880.

8 The Scott Paper Company / was / the first producer / of modern toilet paper.

9 But the company / didn't put / its name / on the product.

10 Today there / are / over 5,000 different companies / producing toilet paper / around the world.

01 Cook with the Sun

쉬운 독해를 위한 Vocabulary 업그레이드

A 다음 영어 표현을 읽고 뜻을 쓰시오.

1	pot	______	9	mirror	______
2	solar	______	10	depend	______
3	trap	______	11	degree	______
4	metal	______	12	reach	______
5	escape	______	13	electricity	______
6	reflective	______	14	outside	______
7	prevent	______	15	principle	______
8	vegetable	______	16	Celsius	______

B 다음 주어진 표현을 배열하여 우리말을 영어로 쓰시오.

1 그녀는 냄비에 준비한 모든 것을 담는다.
(everything / gets / she / a pot / in / ready)

2 거울이나 반사하는 금속이 더 많은 햇빛을 가두는 데 사용된다.
(a mirror / used / to / trap / or reflective metal / is / more sunlight)

3 그러면 유리 뚜껑은 냄비 안의 열이 빠져나가는 것을 막는다.
(a glass cover / escaping / then prevents / heat / inside the pot / from)

4 그녀는 음식을 조리하기 위해서 전기나 가스를 사용할 필요가 없다.
(to cook / her food / need / to use / she / doesn't / any electricity / or gas)

끊어 읽기 구문 학습으로 독해 실력 업그레이드

Study Date: /

C

다음과 같이 끊어진 표시에 유의하여 읽고, 문장을 우리말로 해석하시오.

1 It / is / a cool, but sunny day. // Ms. Green / is ready / to cook / her dinner.

2 She / opens / the door of her home / and goes outside.

3 Then / she / goes / to a park / to play / with her children.

4 When / she / comes back, / dinner / will be waiting / for her.

5 The principle / of solar cooking / is / simple.

6 She / puts / a dark pot / in a sunny place. // The pot / takes in / sunlight.

7 The sunlight / changes / into / heat. // How / hot / will / the pot / get?

8 It / depends, / but / with enough sunlight, / the pot / can reach / 150 degrees Celsius.

9 She / can cook / vegetables, rice, fish, / and even meat.

10 She / doesn't have to heat up / the house / on hot summer days, / either.

02 Carbon Footprint

쉬운 독해를 위한 Vocabulary 업그레이드

A 다음 영어 표현을 읽고 뜻을 쓰시오.

1 product ____________
2 term ____________
3 footprint ____________
4 sum ____________
5 primary ____________
6 emission ____________
7 measure ____________
8 destroy ____________
9 weigh ____________
10 secondary ____________
11 direct ____________
12 cycle ____________
13 create ____________
14 transportation ____________
15 fuel ____________
16 not only A but also B ____________

B 다음 주어진 표현을 배열하여 우리말을 영어로 쓰시오.

1 탄소 발자국은 한 제품이 얼마나 많은 온실가스를 배출하는지 보여준다.
(the carbon / shows / how much / greenhouse gases / a product / footprint / creates)

2 그것은 제품을 만들 때 뿐 아니라 제품을 유지하고 파기할 때도 이루어진다. (but also / from maintaining and / it / not only from making products / destroying them / is created)

3 다음 단계는 이산화탄소를 덜 배출하는 제품을 선택하는 것이다.
(is / less CO_2 emissions / choose products / the next step / that cause / to)

4 하나의 종이컵은 대략 그것의 두 배에 해당하는 온실 가스를 만들어 낸다.
(cup / about twice / its weight / creates / a paper / greenhouse gases)

끊어 읽기 구문 학습으로 독해 실력 업그레이드

Study Date: ____ / ____

C

다음과 같이 끊어진 표시에 유의하여 읽고, 문장을 우리말로 해석하시오.

1 Every single thing / you buy / at a supermarket / creates / greenhouse gases.

2 For example, / a paper cup / weighs / only 5 grams, / but it / produces / 11 grams of greenhouse gases.

3 A kiwifruit / creates / greenhouse gases / five times its own weight / to get to your country / from New Zealand.

4 To measure the amount / of greenhouse gases / created / by a product, / people / use / the term “carbon footprint.”

5 It / is / the sum of two parts, / the primary footprint / and the secondary footprint.

6 The primary footprint / measures / the direct CO_2 emissions / from burning fuels / for production and transportation.

7 The secondary footprint / measures / the indirect CO_2 emissions / from the whole life cycle / of a product.

8 Now you / know / how much greenhouse gases / a product / can create.

9 By shopping / more carefully, / you / can help save / the planet.

01 The Legend of Hanuman

쉬운 독해를 위한 Vocabulary 업그레이드

A

다음 영어 표현을 읽고 뜻을 쓰시오.

1 legend ________

2 temple ________

3 forest ________

4 faraway ________

5 kingdom ________

6 bravely ________

7 rescue ________

8 everywhere ________

9 bring ________

10 especially ________

11 demon ________

12 together ________

13 fight ________

14 search ________

15 because of ________

16 once upon a time ________

B

다음 주어진 표현을 배열하여 우리말을 영어로 쓰시오.

1 그 이유를 설명하는 전설이 있다.
(there / that / explains / is / a legend / why)

2 옛날에, Rama 신과 그의 아내 Sita가 숲에 살았다.
(a time, / the god Rama lived / upon / forest / in the / once / and / his wife Sita)

3 그들은 Hanuman이라는 이름의 날아다니는 원숭이를 만났다.
(they / monkey / whose / met / a flying / name / was / Hanuman)

4 Hanuman은 Rama가 자신의 아내 Sita를 구하는 것을 도왔다.
(Rama / save / his / Hanuman / helped / wife Sita)

끊어 읽기 구문 학습으로 독해 실력 업그레이드

Study Date: /

C

다음과 같이 끊어진 표시에 유의하여 읽고, 문장을 우리말로 해석하시오.

1 In Thailand, / monkeys / are / special animals. // People / are especially kind / to monkeys in temples.

2 Every day / people / bring / food for the monkeys. // They / think / it will bring them / good luck.

3 Why / are / monkeys / so special / in Thailand?

4 One day / a demon / came from / a faraway land / and took Sita / to his kingdom.

5 Sita / was / beautiful, / so the demon / wanted / to marry her.

6 Rama and his brother / searched for / Sita / everywhere, / but / they / couldn't find / her.

7 He / was / clever and strong. // He / wanted / to help Rama.

8 Soon / Hanuman / found out / that the demon / had taken / Sita / to the Island of Lanka.

9 The monkey / fought / bravely / to rescue Sita.

10 Because of this, / Hanuman / became / a hero / across Thailand.

02 On the Elephant's Back

쉬운 독해를 위한 Vocabulary 업그레이드

A

다음 영어 표현을 읽고 뜻을 쓰시오.

1	scenery	______	9	shout	______
2	spend	______	10	strength	______
3	back	______	11	handle	______
4	suddenly	______	12	scream	______
5	sway	______	13	shout	______
6	tear	______	14	ladder	______
7	forward	______	15	sigh of relief	______
8	holiday	______	16	from side to side	______

B

다음 주어진 표현을 배열하여 우리말을 영어로 쓰시오.

1 나는 코끼리 등에 오르기 위해 오래된 사다리를 타고 올라가야 했다.
(I / an ancient / to the elephant's back / to / had / to / climb up / get up / ladder)

2 두려움으로 나는 천천히 코끼리 등에 있는 의자에 앉았다.
(heart, / I / on the seat / sat down / slowly / on / with / fear / in my / its back)

3 나는 양옆으로 흔들렸다.
(from / side / I / swayed / to / side)

4 나는 의자 손잡이를 잡느라고 온 힘을 다 쏟아 부었다.
(I / holding / the handle / put / all my strength / into / on / the seat)

끊어 읽기 구문 학습으로 독해 실력 업그레이드

Study Date: /

C

다음과 같이 끊어진 표시에 유의하여 읽고, 문장을 우리말로 해석하시오.

1 Last week, / my family / spent / our holidays in Thailand. // I / enjoyed / the food and beautiful scenery.

2 I / also enjoyed / whitewater rafting / and hiking in the jungle.

3 But / there was / one thing / I / enjoy. // It / was / riding an elephant!

4 On a bright morning, / I / stood directly / beside one of these huge animals / for the first time / in my life.

5 When / the driver / shouted into / the elephant's ear, / the elephant / suddenly moved / forward.

6 The elephant / was just walking, / but / I / felt like / it was moving / very quickly.

7 After walking / through the forest, / we / finally stopped.

8 A huge sigh of relief / came out of / me. // I / was almost in tears.

9 The driver / asked, / "Do you / want / one more round?" // I / screamed, / "NOOOO!"

01 Muscles at Work

쉬운 독해를 위한 Vocabulary 업그레이드

A 다음 영어 표현을 읽고 뜻을 쓰시오.

1 hundred ______________

2 neck ______________

3 alone ______________

4 skeletal ______________

5 fasten ______________

6 pull ______________

7 elbow ______________

8 pupil ______________

9 notice ______________

10 combination ______________

11 smooth ______________

12 straighten ______________

13 take turns ______________

14 in pairs ______________

15 at work ______________

16 turn around ______________

B 다음 주어진 표현을 배열하여 우리말을 영어로 쓰시오.

1 골격근은 너의 눈동자가 커질 때 작동하지 않는다.
(bigger / pupils / work / skeletal muscles / don't / get / when / your)

2 그것들은 당신을 웃게 하고, 눈을 감게 하고, 음식을 먹게 한다.
(laugh, / close / eat / food / your / eyes, / they / let / you / and)

3 골격근이라 불리는 어떤 근육들은 뼈에 붙어 있다.
(some of /to / bones / muscles, / are / the muscles, / called skeletal / fastened)

4 다른 민무늬근들은 몸을 통해 피가 흐르는 것을 돕는다.
(others / body / move / through / help / the blood / your)

끊어 읽기 구문 학습으로 독해 실력 업그레이드

Study Date: /

C

다음과 같이 끊어진 표시에 유의하여 읽고, 문장을 우리말로 해석하시오.

1 Each person / has / more than / six hundred muscles. // They / are / all over your body.

2 Interestingly, / about one hundred of them / are / in your face / and neck alone.

3 They / usually work / in pairs / because / a muscle / can only pull, / but not push.

4 Skeletal muscles / take turns / pulling bones / when / you / bend / and straighten your elbow / or / when you open / and close your mouth.

5 There are / also / smooth muscles. // They / work / without your thinking / about them.

6 For example, / smooth muscles / in your eyes / change / the size of your pupils.

7 Other smooth muscles / help / your body / make use of the food / you eat.

8 Muscles / work / for you / in special ways, / sometimes / alone / and sometimes / in combination.

9 Even though / you / may not notice / it / or think about it, / they / are always / at work.

02 Exercise in Space

쉬운 독해를 위한 Vocabulary 업그레이드

A

다음 영어 표현을 읽고 뜻을 쓰시오.

1 force ______________
2 fight ______________
3 exercise ______________
4 outer ______________
5 strap ______________
6 machine ______________
7 buckle ______________
8 wheel ______________
9 float ______________
10 weak ______________
11 similar ______________
12 space ______________
13 gravity ______________
14 treadmill ______________
15 astronaut ______________
16 stay healthy ______________

B

다음 주어진 표현을 배열하여 우리말을 영어로 쓰시오.

1 우리는 중력과 싸우기 위해 근육과 뼈를 이용한다.
(muscles / to fight / and bones / use / we / gravity)

2 근육과 뼈들이 쉽게 약해질 수 있다.
(can / easily become / muscles / and bones / weak)

3 그것이 우주비행사들이 건강을 유지하기 위해 날마다 운동해야 하는 이유이다.
(that / every day / to / stay / is / why / astronauts / have / to / exercise / healthy)

4 그들은 그 기계 장치에 그들 자신을 끈으로 묶어야 한다.
(they / have / to / the machine / to / strap / themselves)

끊어 읽기 구문 학습으로 독해 실력 업그레이드

Study Date: ______ / ______

C

다음과 같이 끊어진 표시에 유의하여 읽고, 문장을 우리말로 해석하시오.

1 On Earth, / even during sleep, / the human body / moves / against the force of gravity.

2 Thus, / our body / always gets / lots of exercise.

3 In space, / however, / the human body / doesn't have to fight / gravity / because / outer space / is free / from gravity.

4 Exercise / is / one of the most important things / they do / during their time in space.

5 To exercise, / astronauts / use / machines / such as treadmills / and special bikes.

6 They / run / on the treadmill. // Because / there is / no gravity / in space, / they / can float / in the air.

7 The exercise bike, / called the cycle ergometer, / is / a machine / similar to a bicycle / without wheels.

8 They / strap / their shoes / into buckles / and / wear seat belts / to hold themselves down.

9 If / astronauts / don't exercise enough / in space, / they / may have / a hard time / getting used to life back / on Earth.

01 Living Alone

쉬운 독해를 위한 Vocabulary 업그레이드

A

다음 영어 표현을 읽고 뜻을 쓰시오.

1	trend	________	9	rate	________
2	report	________	10	percentage	________
3	research	________	11	population	________
4	nearly	________	12	direction	________
5	overall	________	13	household	________
6	expert	________	14	divorce	________
7	predict	________	15	for instance	________
8	developed	________	16	according to	________

B

다음 주어진 표현을 배열하여 우리말을 영어로 쓰시오.

1 점점 더 많은 사람들이 혼자 살고 있다.
(more / living / alone / and / more / people / are)

2 그 비율은 대도시에서 훨씬 더 높다.
(in / big/ much / higher / cities / the rate / is)

3 그 비율은 개발도상국에서는 훨씬 낮다.
(the rate/ developing/ lower / in / nations / is / far)

4 전문가들은 그 추세가 계속될 것이라고 전망한다.
(will / predict / the trend / continue / experts)

끊어 읽기 구문 학습으로 독해 실력 업그레이드

Study Date: /

C

다음과 같이 끊어진 표시에 유의하여 읽고, 문장을 우리말로 해석하시오.

1 The single-person household / is / a growing trend.

2 According to Euromonitor, / a research company / in the United Kingdom, / the number of single-person households in the world / went up / by 33 percent / in just ten years.

3 The report / also says / that almost one / in every ten households / has / just one person.

4 In France, / nearly half of / the population in Paris / lives / alone.

5 Overall, / the percentage of single-person households / is / far greater / in developed nations.

6 For example, / one in three households / in the United States / has just one person.

7 In South America, / for instance, / only about 7% of all households / are single-person.

8 People / live / longer, / and the number of older people / who live alone / is increasing.

9 Also, people / tend / to marry later, / and divorce / is / becoming more common.

10 For various reasons, / more people / are choosing / to live alone.

02 Convenience Foods

쉬운 독해를 위한 Vocabulary 업그레이드

A 다음 영어 표현을 읽고 뜻을 쓰시오.

1 need ______________
2 easily ______________
3 among ______________
4 popular ______________
5 tasty ______________
6 freeze ______________
7 nutrient ______________
8 technology ______________
9 meat ______________
10 fresh ______________
11 twice ______________
12 contain ______________
13 convenience ______________
14 chemical ______________
15 microwave oven ______________
16 thanks to ______________

B 다음 주어진 표현을 배열하여 우리말을 영어로 쓰시오.

1 그것들은 항상 구입하기 쉽고 사용 가능하다.
(buy / are / and ready / easy / to / they / always / to use)

2 몇 분 동안 전자레인지에 그것들을 넣으면, 여러분은 맛있는 식사를 할 것이다.
(put / you / them / will have / a tasty meal / in your microwave / a few minutes, / and / oven / for)

3 그것들은 일반적으로 많은 소금과 화학 물질을 포함하고 있다.
(they / a / of / salt / usually / lot / contain / and chemicals)

4 그것들은 또한 특별한 용기에 음식을 신선하게 유지할 수 있다.
(they / fresh / in / can / packages / foods / special / also keep)

끊어 읽기 구문 학습으로 독해 실력 업그레이드

Study Date: /

C

다음과 같이 끊어진 표시에 유의하여 읽고, 문장을 우리말로 해석하시오.

1 As / more and more people / are living / alone, / there is / growing need / for foods / that can be easily cooked.

2 These foods / are called / "convenience foods." // They / come / in small packages.

3 Convenience foods / are becoming / popular / among people / who live alone / or / have little time / to cook.

4 Thanks to / new technology, / people / can freeze / vegetables, fruit, meat, and fish / without losing their nutrients much.

5 However, / convenience foods / have / some problems / because / the foods / are less healthy.

6 Many of them / contain / more salt / than the food / you make at home.

7 Also, / they / often include / more chemicals / that may not be good / for your health.

8 So, / read / food labels / carefully.

9 Also, / you / should not eat / convenience foods / more than / twice a week.

UNIT 12

01 Writing a Book Report

쉬운 독해를 위한 Vocabulary 업그레이드

A 다음 영어 표현을 읽고 뜻을 쓰시오.

1 author ____________

2 step ____________

3 prepare ____________

4 favorite ____________

5 follow ____________

6 solution ____________

7 decide ____________

8 information ____________

9 opinion ____________

10 common ____________

11 remember ____________

12 recommend ____________

13 paragraph ____________

14 summarize ____________

15 such as ____________

16 take note ____________

B 다음 주어진 표현을 배열하여 우리말을 영어로 쓰시오.

1 그것은 또한 책에 대한 의견도 제공한다.
(an / book / opinion / about / it / also gives / the)

2 당신이 그 책에 관심이 있다면, 훨씬 더 쉽게 책을 이해할 수 있다. (if / you / understand / it / are / interested / in the book, / you / can / much more easily)

3 세 번째, 그 이야기를 요약하는 단락을 써라.
(paragraph / the story / third, / summarizing / write / a /)

4 당신이 가장 좋아하는 부분이나 알게 된 것을 쓸 수 있다.
(you / part / or what / can / write / about / your / favorite / you / learned)

끊어 읽기 구문 학습으로 독해 실력 업그레이드

Study Date: /

C

다음과 같이 끊어진 표시에 유의하여 읽고, 문장을 우리말로 해석하시오.

1 Writing a book report / is / a common problem / for many students.

2 A book report / gives / information / about a book / such as title, author, and a summary / of the book.

3 To write a good book report, / there / are / some important steps / that you need to follow.

4 First of all, / choose / a book / you like. // Second, / take notes / as you read.

5 Prepare / a pen and paper / before you / start / reading / and take notes / about the characters / and main ideas.

6 You / need to write / about the main characters, / their problems, / and their solutions.

7 Lastly, / write / a paragraph / about your opinion / of the book.

8 Remember / that every good report / answers / this important question: / Would you recommend / the book / to others?

9 After reading your report, / people / should be able to decide / if they / want to read / the book.

UNIT 12

02 Around the World in 80 Days

쉬운 독해를 위한 Vocabulary 업그레이드

A 다음 영어 표현을 읽고 뜻을 쓰시오.

1 novel ______________
2 argue ______________
3 rich ______________
4 bet ______________
5 steam ______________
6 arrive ______________
7 expect ______________
8 sleigh ______________
9 yacht ______________
10 later ______________
11 gain ______________
12 however ______________
13 whether ______________
14 science ______________
15 adventure ______________
16 be based on ______________

B 다음 주어진 표현을 배열하여 우리말을 영어로 쓰시오.

1 그것은 단지 80일 만에 세계 일주를 했던 사람에 대한 이야기이다.
(it / who / in / only / is / a man / world / went / 80 days / the / about / around)

2 그는 런던에 살았던 부자였다.
(a / rich / he / lived / man / London / was / in / who)

3 그는 그가 예상했던 것보다 몇 분 뒤에 집에 도착했다.
(he / a few / he / minutes / later / than / arrived / home / expected)

4 그것은 또한 과학에 근거를 둔 것이다.
(it / based / science, / too / is / on)

끊어 읽기 구문 학습으로 독해 실력 업그레이드

Study Date: /

C 다음과 같이 끊어진 표시에 유의하여 읽고, 문장을 우리말로 해석하시오.

1 *Around the World in 80 Days* / is / an adventure novel / by Jules Verne.

2 His name / was / Phileas Fogg. // One day, / he / argued / with his friends / about whether / a man / could go / around the world / in 80 days.

3 He / bet / £20,000 / that he could do it.

4 Traveling around the world in 80 days / is not / a problem today.

5 But / there were / no airplanes / at that time.

6 Mr. Fogg / had to ride / trains, steam boats, yachts, sleighs, / and even elephants.

7 He / thought / he had lost / all his money. // But there / was / one more day left.

8 The idea / that Mr. Fogg gained one day / was / my favorite part / of the book.

9 He / gained / one day / because he / traveled / east / and crossed / the International Date Line.

10 This / is / the part / that makes / the book / not just an adventure story.

01 Egyptian Way to Multiply

쉬운 독해를 위한 Vocabulary 업그레이드

A

다음 영어 표현을 읽고 뜻을 쓰시오.

1 method ____________

2 suppose ____________

3 double ____________

4 multiply ____________

5 calculate ____________

6 opposite ____________

7 underline ____________

8 especially ____________

9 case ____________

10 allow ____________

11 add up ____________

12 without ____________

13 a piece of ____________

14 calculator ____________

15 and so on ____________

16 multiplication table ____________

B

다음 주어진 표현을 배열하여 우리말을 영어로 쓰시오.

1 구구단(곱셈표)은 우리가 쉽게 숫자를 계산할 수 있게 한다.
(the multiplication / allows / us / to / calculate / table / numbers easily)

2 종이 한 장에 세로선을 그린다.
(a / piece / down / of / paper / draw / a line)

3 숫자 2, 4, 8의 합은 14이다.
(the numbers / to / 14 / 2, 4, and 8 / add / up)

4 이 숫자들을 더하라, 그러면 392를 얻을 것이다.
(add / will / get / 392 / these / numbers, / and / you)

끊어 읽기 구문 학습으로 독해 실력 업그레이드

Study Date: /

C 다음과 같이 끊어진 표시에 유의하여 읽고, 문장을 우리말로 해석하시오.

1 When we / multiply / numbers / without a calculator, / we / use / the multiplication table.

2 But ancient Egyptians / used / another method, / especially for large numbers.

3 Suppose / you / have / this problem: 14 x 28 = ?

4 On the left side, / write / 1, 2, 4, 8, 16, / and so on.

5 On the right side, / write / the number / you are multiplying by (in this case, 28).

6 Under 28, / write 56. // That / is / double 28.

7 Then double / 56, / and write / the number 112 / under it. // Keep / going. // Your table / should look like / this:

8 Now find / the numbers / on the left side / that add up / to the first number / in the problem (in this case, 14).

9 Then underline / the numbers / on the right side / opposite these numbers / (in this case, 56, 112, and 224).

10 This / is / the answer to 14 x 28.

02 Learning Multiplication

쉬운 독해를 위한 Vocabulary 업그레이드

A

다음 영어 표현을 읽고 뜻을 쓰시오.

1 pattern ____________

2 equal ____________

3 divide ____________

4 result ____________

5 together ____________

6 notice ____________

7 memorize ____________

8 carefully ____________

9 same ____________

10 property ____________

11 sum ____________

12 times ____________

13 mean ____________

14 multiplication ____________

15 in a row ____________

16 figure out ____________

B

다음 주어진 표현을 배열하여 우리말을 영어로 쓰시오.

1 당신이 주의를 기울여 그것을 보면, 몇몇 흥미로운 패턴을 발견할 수 있다.
(you / if / at / it / look / can / carefully, / you / some / interesting / patterns / find)

2 그것들을 다섯 개짜리 묶음으로 나누어 보라.
(into / groups / divide / them / of / five)

3 당신은 A 곱하기 B는 항상 B 곱하기 A라는 것을 알 수 있다.
(that / A×B / can / find / as / B×A / is / always / the same / you)

4 여기서 무슨 일이 일어나고 있는지 이해할 수 있는가?
(can / is / going / on / you / figure / out / what / here?)

끊어 읽기 구문 학습으로 독해 실력 업그레이드

Study Date: /

C 다음과 같이 끊어진 표시에 유의하여 읽고, 문장을 우리말로 해석하시오.

1 In Korea, / students / usually memorize / the multiplication table.

2 From the multiplication table, / you / can notice / that 3×5 equals 5×3. // Wonder / why?

3 3×5 / means / you / have / five groups / of three.

4 Put / the five groups / together. // How many / do / you / have? // Yes, 3×5 = 15.

5 How many groups / do / you / have? Yes, / you / have / three groups of five.

6 This / means / that you / only have to / memorize / half of the numbers / in the table.

7 Here / is / another interesting pattern.

8 The results / in the 9 times table / (the red numbers in a row) / have / a special property: / for each result of / 9 × a one-digit number, / the sum / of the digits / is / 9.

9 Here / is / one more fun pattern. // Multiplication by 11 / is / very easy.

10 Add / the two digits / and place / the sum / in between them.

01 If I Look at the One

쉬운 독해를 위한 Vocabulary 업그레이드

A 다음 영어 표현을 읽고 뜻을 쓰시오.

1 once ______________
2 mass ______________
3 conduct ______________
4 total ______________
5 researcher ______________
6 receive ______________
7 average ______________
8 statistics ______________
9 complete ______________
10 result ______________
11 million ______________
12 fill out ______________
13 willingness ______________
14 electronic product ______________
15 in exchange for ______________
16 on the other hand ______________

B 다음 주어진 표현을 배열하여 우리말을 영어로 쓰시오.

1 그 설문 조사는 다양한 전자 제품 사용에 관한 것이었다.
(their / use / of / different / the survey / was / about / electronic / products)

2 조사가 끝난 후, 각각의 학생은 5달러와 편지 한 통을 받았다.
(after / given / $5 / completing / the survey, / each / student / was / and / a letter)

3 그들은 집에 가기 전에 편지를 주의 깊게 읽을 것을 요구 받았다.
(they /carefully / before / were / asked / to / read / the letter / going / home)

4 그들은 원한다면 돈을 기부할 수 있었다.
(they / they / wanted / could / donate / money / if)

끊어 읽기 구문 학습으로 독해 실력 업그레이드

Study Date: /

C

다음과 같이 끊어진 표시에 유의하여 읽고, 문장을 우리말로 해석하시오.

1 Mother Teresa / once said, / "If / I / look at / the mass, / I / will never act. // If / I / look at / the one, / I / will."

2 She / meant / that willingness to help others / begins / with one person.

3 Some researchers / wanted / to test / this idea, / so in 2007 / they / conducted / a study.

4 A total / of 121 students / at an American university / were asked / to fill out / a short survey / in exchange for $5.

5 One / showed / statistics: / 3 million hungry children / in Malawi / and 11 million hungry children / in Ethiopia.

6 The other / only showed / stories about Rokia, a poor / and hungry girl / from Mali, Africa.

7 The results / were / very different.

8 People / who received / the statistics / donated / an average of $1.17.

9 On the other hand, / people who learned / about Rokia / donated / an average of $2.83.

02 Knit One, Save One

쉬운 독해를 위한 Vocabulary 업그레이드

A

다음 영어 표현을 읽고 뜻을 쓰시오.

1 newborn ____________
2 within ____________
3 critical ____________
4 birth ____________
5 reach ____________
6 provide ____________
7 infection ____________
8 donation ____________
9 soap ____________
10 knit ____________
11 collect ____________
12 successful ____________
13 campaign ____________
14 handmade ____________
15 several ____________
16 handwashing ____________

B

다음 주어진 표현을 배열하여 우리말을 영어로 쓰시오.

1 아기의 머리에 작은 모자를 씌워주는 것이 아기의 생명을 구할 수 있다.
(putting / a / save/ its / life / little / cap / on / a baby's / head / can)

2 그 캠페인은 사람들에게 아프리카의 신생아들을 위한 모자를 뜨개질해 달라고 요청했다.
(asked / people / a cap / for / newborn / the campaign / to / knit / African babies)

3 만약 여러분이 손뜨개에 능숙하지 못하다면, 여러분은 10달러를 보냄으로써 아기들을 구할 수 있다.
(at / if / good /knitting, / you / can / babies / by / you / are / not / save / sending $10)

4 그 비누는 아기들을 감염되지 않도록 지키는 데 도움이 될 것이다.
(the soap / of / infections / will / help / keep / the baby / free)

끊어 읽기 구문 학습으로 독해 실력 업그레이드

Study Date: /

C

다음과 같이 끊어진 표시에 유의하여 읽고, 문장을 우리말로 해석하시오.

1 Most people / think / that it / is / hot / in Africa.

2 But even in Africa, / keeping a newborn baby warm / during the first critical days / is / very important.

3 Every year / nearly 4 million babies / in Africa / lose / their lives / within a month / after birth.

4 Save the Children, / an independent organization / for helping children, / started / its "Knit One, Save One" campaign / in 2007.

5 It / was / successful / in several countries, / such as Germany, the U.S., the UK, and South Korea.

6 For example, / 25,000 knitted caps / were collected / in South Korea / in the first year.

7 In the next year, / the number / reached / more than 80,000.

8 With ten dollars, / you / can provide / a handmade cap / and soap for handwashing.

9 Babies / are / the same / all across the world, / and each baby / has / the right to have a healthy start.

10 Remember, / just a small donation / can save / a baby's life.

01 Pyramids in Mexico and Egypt

쉬운 독해를 위한 Vocabulary 업그레이드

A

다음 영어 표현을 읽고 뜻을 쓰시오.

1 modern ____________
2 pointed ____________
3 narrow ____________
4 worship ____________
5 shape ____________
6 heaven ____________
7 passage ____________
8 technology ____________
9 soul ____________
10 purpose ____________
11 connect ____________
12 mummy ____________
13 structure ____________
14 blood ____________
15 lead to ____________
16 thousands of ____________

B

다음 주어진 표현을 배열하여 우리말을 영어로 쓰시오.

1 멕시코의 피라미드는 형태와 구조면에서 이집트의 것과는 다르다.
(pyramids / are / ones / in / shape / different / from / the Egyptian / the Mexican / and structure)

2 좁은 통로가 그 방을 피라미드의 꼭대기와 연결한다.
(a narrow / to / the top / passage / connects / the / room / of / the pyramid)

3 멕시코의 피라미드는 평평한 꼭대기와 그 꼭대기로 이어지는 계단이 있다.
(a / flat / steps / which / top / and / lead / to / a Mexican pyramid / has / the top)

4 반면에 멕시코의 피라미드는 신을 숭배하기 위해 지어졌다.
(on built / to / worship / the other / hand, / a Mexican / pyramid / was / gods)

끊어 읽기 구문 학습으로 독해 실력 업그레이드

Study Date: ____ / ____

C

다음과 같이 끊어진 표시에 유의하여 읽고, 문장을 우리말로 해석하시오.

1 Almost everyone / knows / that there are / a lot of pyramids / in Egypt.

2 Not many people / know, / however, / that the ancient people / of Mexico / also built / great pyramids.

3 The pyramids / in Mexico / are also large / and wonderful.

4 Thousands of people / worked / for many years / to build them, / and they / did / so / without modern technology.

5 An Egyptian pyramid / has / a pointed top / and a small room / inside.

6 In addition, / the pyramids / had / different purposes.

7 An Egyptian pyramid / was built / to help the pharaoh / to live forever.

8 The mummy of a pharaoh / was laid / inside the small room.

9 Ancient Egyptians / believed / that the pharaoh's soul / could travel / to heaven / through the narrow passage.

10 Ancient Mexicans / walked up / to the flat top / and offered / animal and human blood. They / believed / that their gods / needed / blood for food.

02 The Great Science of Mayans

쉬운 독해를 위한 Vocabulary 업그레이드

A

다음 영어 표현을 읽고 뜻을 쓰시오.

1 symbol ______________

2 central ______________

3 advanced ______________

4 concept ______________

5 aware ______________

6 accurate ______________

7 measure ______________

8 mathematics ______________

9 count ______________

10 astronomy ______________

11 represent ______________

12 vertically ______________

13 civilization ______________

14 length ______________

15 solar year ______________

16 consist of ______________

B

다음 주어진 표현을 배열하여 우리말을 영어로 쓰시오.

1 마야 문명은 0을 사용한 최초의 문명 중 하나였다.
(of / the / earliest / civilizations / Maya / civilization / was / one / to use / zero)

2 그 숫자들은 수직으로 쓰였다.
(were / vertically / written / the / numbers)

3 마야인들은 태양년의 길이도 매우 정확하게 측정했다.
(the Mayans year / very / measured / the / length / of / the solar / accurately)

4 그들은 일 년이 365일보다 조금 더 길다는 것을 인식하고 있었다.
(aware / that / little / longer / they / were / than / 365 days / a year / is / a)

끊어 읽기 구문 학습으로 독해 실력 업그레이드

Study Date: /

C

다음과 같이 끊어진 표시에 유의하여 읽고, 문장을 우리말로 해석하시오.

1 Maya civilization / was / in Central America.

2 During its Classic Period / from A.D. 250 to 900, / it / was / one of the most advanced civilizations / in the world.

3 It / was / especially advanced / in mathematics and astronomy.

4 The concept of zero / plays / a central role / in mathematics, / but most civilizations of the time / did not have / it.

5 The Maya people, / however, / used / a flat, round shape / to represent / zero.

6 They / used / three symbols / to count numbers — / a shell for zero, / a dot for one, / and a line for five.

7 For example, / to represent 13, / three dots / were written / side by side / with two lines under them.

8 In the Mayan calendar, / a year / consists of / 365.242036 days.

9 This / is / slightly more accurate / than the 365.2425 days / of the Gregorian calendar, / which / has been used / since the 16th century.

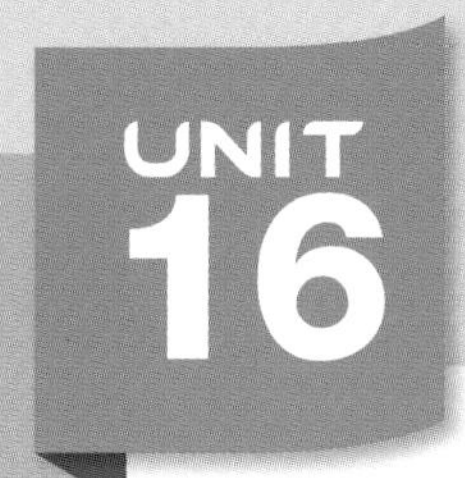

01~02 The Armadillo's Song

쉬운 독해를 위한 Vocabulary 업그레이드

A

다음 영어 표현을 읽고 뜻을 쓰시오.

1 drag ____________
2 rainfall ____________
3 pond ____________
4 cricket ____________
5 bend ____________
6 wizard ____________
7 desire ____________
8 ridiculous ____________
9 creep ____________
10 merrily ____________
11 instrument ____________
12 stare ____________
13 amazement ____________
14 at last ____________
15 be reluctant to ____________
16 laugh at ____________

B

다음 주어진 표현을 배열하여 우리말을 영어로 쓰시오.

1 개구리들은 이 우스운 동물을 비웃었다.
(at / funny animal / the frogs / were / this / laughing)

2 귀뚜라미 가족이 아르마딜로 근처에 있는 새 집으로 이사를 왔다.
(a family / a new house / near / / of crickets / moved / into / the armadillo)

3 아르마딜로는 그 지역에서 가장 훌륭한 마법사를 찾아갔다.
(the armadillo / wizard / in / visited / the / greatest / the / area)

4 마법사는 이렇게 순진한 아르마딜로의 목숨을 빼앗는 게 내키지 않았다.
(the life / reluctant / to / take / of / such / a / the wizard / was / fine / armadillo)

끊어 읽기 구문 학습으로 독해 실력 업그레이드

Study Date: ______ / ______

C

다음과 같이 끊어진 표시에 유의하여 읽고, 문장을 우리말로 해석하시오.

1 There once / lived / an armadillo / who loved music / more than anything else / in the world.

2 After every rainfall, / the armadillo / would drag / his shell / to the large pond.

3 He / would listen to / the big green frogs / singing / to each other / in the most amazing voices.

4 "Oh," / thought / the armadillo, / "how I wish I could sing."

5 "Don't be ridiculous," / sang / the frogs. // "Armadillos / can't sing."

6 He / was amazed to hear / them / sing / as merrily as / the frogs.

7 He / would creep / next to their house / and listen / all day and all night / for their musical sounds.

8 "Oh," / sighed / the armadillo, / "how I wish I could sing."

9 He / said, / "Great wizard, / it / is / my deepest desire to learn / to sing like the frogs and the crickets."

끊어 읽기 구문 학습으로 독해 실력 업그레이드

Study Date: ___ / ___

10 The wizard / bent / low to the ground / and looked / the creature / in the eye.

11 "I / can make / you / sing, / little armadillo," / he said.

12 "But you / do not want / to pay / the price, / for / it / will mean / your death."

13 "You / mean / if I die, / I / will be able to sing?" / asked the armadillo / in amazement. // "Yes, / this / is / so," / said the wizard.

14 "Then, / I / want / to die / right now!" / said the armadillo. // "I / would do / anything / to be able to sing!"

15 But the creature / insisted. // Finally, / the wizard / killed / the armadillo, / made / a musical instrument / from his shell, / and gave / it / to the finest musician / in the town.

16 Sometimes / the musician / would play / his instrument / by the house / where the crickets lived.

17 They / would creep / outside / to stare at him / with big eyes / and say: / "Ai! Ai! // The armadillo / has learned / to sing."

18 And so / it / was. // The armadillo / had learned / to sing / at last, / and his voice / was / the finest / in the land.

조금더
공부해
볼까?

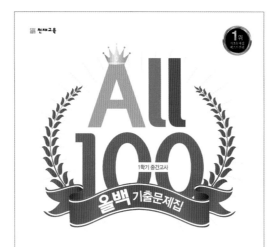